Cormac McCarthy's Western Novels

Cormac McCarthy's Western Novels

BARCLEY OWENS

The University of Arizona Press

TUCSON

First printing
The University of Arizona Press
© 2000 The Arizona Board of Regents
All rights reserved
♾ This book is printed on acid-free, archival-quality paper.
Manufactured in the United States of America

05 04 03 02 01 00   6 5 4 3 2 1

Library of Congress Cataloging-in-Publication Data
Owens, Barcley, 1960–
Cormac McCarthy's western novels / Barcley Owens.
p. cm.
Includes bibliographical references.
ISBN 0-8165-1927-7 (acid-free paper) – ISBN 0-8165-1928-5
(pbk.: acid-free paper)
1. McCarthy, Cormac, 1933—Criticism and interpretation. 2. Mexican-American Border Region—In literature. 3. McCarthy, Cormac, 1933—Border trilogy. 4. Western stories—History and criticism. I. Title.
PS3563.C337 Z794   2000
813′.54–dc21
00-008080

British Library Cataloguing-in-Publication Data
A catalogue record for this book is available from the British Library.

To my mother, the memory of my father,
and the continuing love of my family

Contents

Introduction ix

1 *Blood Meridian*'s Violence 3

2 *Blood Meridian* and the Reassessment of Violence 19

3 *Blood Meridian* and Literary Naturalism 45

4 Western Myths in *All the Pretty Horses* and *The Crossing* 63

5 Thematic Motifs in *Cities of the Plain* 97

Afterword 117

Notes 125

Works Cited 129

Introduction

[Do] similar evolutionary forces continue to be at work in chimpanzee and human lineages, maintaining and refining a system of intergroup hostility and personal violence that has existed since even before the ancestors of chimpanzees and humans mated for the last time in a drying forest of eastern Africa around 5 million years ago? If so, one must ask, what forces are they? What bred male bonding and lethal raiding in our forebears and keeps it now in chimpanzees and humans? What marks have those ancient evolutionary forces forged onto our twentieth-century psyches? And what do they say about our hopes and fears for the future?
—Richard Wrangham and Dale Peterson,
Demonic Males: Apes and the Origins of Human Violence

From "historical bedrock" an old story is unearthed in all of its enthralling complexity: scarred bones bearing the unmistakable grooves of tools, spear points and arrowheads, charred ribs from prehistoric barbecues.[1] Every year more of the original script is discovered, what Cormac McCarthy calls "the bones of things."[2] Predatory human violence is far older than we want to imagine. The evidence tells us the story of the hunt and hunted that predates our species, and that may, unavoidably, doom our future. From such primordial beginnings mankind has emerged as the fittest species on earth—number one, on top of the food chain. From out of the African savanna we walked upright, competing, breeding, and most importantly, sitting around campfires, talking, forging tools, making plans. From large rocks and sticks to bolas, spears, and bows, to the sacred metallurgy for knives, swords, and armor, we have kept ourselves well armed, busily subduing the earth. But this violent past portends an apocalyptic future. Our big brain and facile opposable thumb, which so efficiently brought down mammoths, today can put a basketball through a hoop, catch a football, and hit seventy home runs in one season. But they also construct mail bombs, blackpox, and nuclear backpacks. Our well-tooled, dexterous kind has spread like a biological contagion through time, across all continents and into every ecological niche. We have evolved socially—from primal bands to premodern tribes to industrial nations. During the twentieth century, wars of nationalistic fervor have pressed us into service to defend ethnocentric ideologies. Right or wrong, love it or leave it, we have killed our own kind by the millions. Patriotism has pushed the buttons of the atomic age and built the smokestacks of industry. Loyalties have evolved along with our social institutions: we defend our family, our neighborhood, our community, our state, our nation. Since the breakup of the Soviet Union, we have witnessed a return to ethnic tribalism: Croatians killing Serbs killing Albanians. The questing urge to see what's beyond the next ridge has always included killing what we find there, whether it is useful for food or dangerous or simply different. After all of our civilized progress, how far removed are we from the dimly lit cave in Spain now known as Gran Dolina, roughly 800,000 years ago, when a "small party of humans" sitting next to a campfire stripped meat off bones, wielded stone knives and hammers, and snapped vertebrae to get at the protein-rich marrow (Kunzig 91)? How different are we? Indeed, what were they thinking that night as they sat around the campfire eating fresh kill, the "rag doll" corpses of "an eleven-year-old boy or girl" and "a couple of toddlers of three or four" (90–91)?

This is the world of Cormac McCarthy's *Blood Meridian*. And more than any other contemporary American novel, it forces us to examine that world head-on. McCarthy prompts us to ask ourselves why, for instance, we watch Quentin Tarantino films or Jerry Springer, or why our national attention is riveted to real-life violence, such as the O.J. trial, the Timothy McVeigh trial, the JonBenet Ramsey investigation, or whatever the most recent mayhem might be. Our fascination and horror are twinned, paradoxical responses, compelling us to keep watching, to

INTRODUCTION

satiate our desire for a vicarious thrill. Robert D. Kaplan likens such media fare to the extreme violence of the Roman Colosseum and condemns it as America's equivalent of "gladiator entertainments" ("Was Democracy" 79). If we are to understand this violent American video culture, we need to subject our national pastimes—sports, news, TV, films—to some hard questions. Our daily bread of mass-media culture—from "My McDonald's" advertising to *Monday Night Football*—keeps us from thinking clearly and encourages us, rather, as Nike says, to "Just do it," which always means, "Buy this product." Our perceptions of everything American are obscured by our very participation in "my America." As we curse the traffic, turn up the gangster rap, pick up an action video, eat a triple cheeseburger, and rush home to watch the playoffs, we ignore our origins. Living in what many call a postmodern culture, we seem far removed from howls in the night, the smell of blood, and the taste of raw meat on the bone.

Some critics have grouped *Blood Meridian* with *All the Pretty Horses, The Crossing,* and *Cities of the Plain,* labeling them all as postmodern westerns. This generalization shows how common the word *postmodern* has become, how it is currently a worn cliché, a synonym for everything *contemporary*. *Blood Meridian* is quite different from the Border Trilogy. The first of McCarthy's westerns, it is also the last of his gothic novels, a historical novel of grotesque images and atavistic violence. Published in 1986, the book is a product of its post-Vietnam era. In stark contrast, the Border Trilogy is grounded in the nostalgic, mythic remembrance of the Old West and American cowboys. In no way can McCarthy's last three novels seriously be considered postmodern. Postmodernists gesture toward the American West as an ironic signifier of American imperialism, an embarrassing point in American history when greed and wanderlust led to large-scale land grabbing and genocide of native peoples. To a postmodernist, the American West is yet another mythos for parody and mock heroics, as in Thomas Pynchon's *Gravity's Rainbow* or Thomas Berger's *Little Big Man*. By nature urban, contemporary, and experimental, postmodernists do not locate their characters and themes within the narrow mythic world of the Old West. They employ cultural images as gestures, often juxtaposing pop-culture allusions in high-energy montages with improvisational adrenaline speed, like rock guitarists riffing off chords. (Consider the prose of Kathy Acker, Sherman Alexie, Ann Beattie, William S. Burroughs, T. Coraghessan Boyle, Don DeLillo, Joyce Carol Oates, Toni Morrison, Ishmael Reed, Hunter S. Thompson, Tom Wolfe, or even Stephen King, for that matter.) Thumb through any anthology or journal and you will likely find that more than half of the authors may be described as postmodernists, both in inclination and technique. McCarthy should not be labeled as one of their ilk. Rather, he is a regionalist—first a Southern writer, a native of Tennessee, and since the publication of *Blood Meridian* a western writer who has adopted the Texas border and its aesthetics. Like other cowboy heroes, the boys of the Border Trilogy are young guns, two-fisted, adventuresome rebels who prove to be unlucky in love. Their first love remains the hardscrabble life of a working cowboy: an honest day's work, a well-bred horse, a home-cooked meal, a blood-red sunset, and row upon row of distant snow-capped peaks. This is hardly the stuff of postmodern culture.

Blood Meridian is more difficult to classify. Because it is set in the Old West and graphically details the killing of Indians and Mexicans and Whites, some critics categorize it as historical revisionism or postmodern romance. My own examination of this significant novel cuts for sign across several domains: the varying critical responses, the Vietnam era's reassessment of violence, and literary naturalism. Throughout the novel, McCarthy's characters—especially Judge Holden and the kid—relentlessly play out the old pursuit of predator and prey. The trail of *Blood Meridian* is a blood trail, receding back as far as the eye can see, to the dawn of mankind, of all life, and reaching perhaps to faraway horizons of men yet to come. *Blood Meridian* deserves closer scrutiny: it is McCarthy's best work, his magnum opus, and one of American literature's darkest odysseys into the westering impulse. The novel justly continues to receive far more critical attention than any of his other works.

Some early reviewers of *Blood Meridian* found the narrative voice overwritten, turgid, even purple. Most readers, myself included, find the book not only readable but enticingly full of ornate gestures and tidbits of arcane detail. A layering of tonalities, as found in the resonating dream sequences or landscape descriptions, has the ability to radiate experiences beyond our conscious power to understand. McCarthy's prose gushes like a river, violent as whitewater in places, dreamy and placid elsewhere; but

INTRODUCTION

always underneath, the thematic tow is swift and deep. So deep that we can't always see the bottom. If we are fishing for critical approaches, we know there may be all sorts of interesting trout in the text, down in there somewhere, but efforts to tease them out, to tie just the right fly, mostly fail. McCarthy is doing what he wants according to his own agenda, mixing various cultural sources and old voices, shocking us with inappropriate comedy and horrifying us with a litany of corpses. In this respect his art imitates his life—critics, casual readers, and devoted fans be damned. And he is not going to grant us absolution or bother explaining matters, large or small, within his books. There will be no authorial exegesis, no addendum, no lectures, no interviews. What we get, instead, is the thrill of the ride and sights that leave us dumbstruck, tingling, guilty in our participation. In *Blood Meridian* we are part of a great literary crime, a strange drama in which the devil fiddles, dances, grins, and wins while the rest of humanity remains ignorant of the proceedings. And none of the "Yes, but's" about the book as a historical romance or moral parable or epic tragedy will suffice. We have gotten our money's worth from a writer so talented he can make us laugh at images of extreme depredation. Certain scenes in *Blood Meridian,* like Captain White's head in the jar of mescal, are cinematic, fusing the bizarre and brutal into shocking, grotesque juxtaposition. And our own rueful laughs tell us more about ourselves than we want to admit. We are caught vicariously participating in a spectacle of gross sensationalism—bingeing on adrenaline, sweating, laughing. Despite attempts to sneak back later, to redact the evidence, to investigate our reactions, to explain away certain scenes as moral, we cannot forget the initial shock of the novel's violence. We can try every fly in our academic hats, plumb every intertextual hole in search of beautiful fish, but after such analysis, we certainly end up with less than we begin with on that first wild ride down the river.

Although Cormac McCarthy's fortunes have skyrocketed with the publication of the Border Trilogy, several aspects of his life have mostly kept him out of the public eye. First, he does not advertise himself—no book-signing tours, no talk shows, no readings, no academic attachments, no interviews. This is indeed rare in the highly networked and publicity-seeking world of publishing. A second factor has been the long gaps between novels, which average several years. A third, and more serious, hindrance has been the extreme violence of his earlier work, reaching a shocking crescendo in *Blood Meridian*. For better or worse, this last quality changed in 1992 with *All the Pretty Horses,* which was awarded the National Book Award and made the *New York Times* bestseller list, becoming that most esteemed of literary creations, a popular novel with serious artistic merit. A small cadre of scholars, "like the disciples of a new faith" (to borrow the ex-priest Tobin's description of Glanton's gang), now make the pilgrimage to McCarthy conferences, and the critical discourse is evolving into a specialized field of inquiry known as McCarthy studies.[3] No longer do his fans have to answer the puzzled bookstore clerk's query, "Which McCarthy?" Although the author has not changed his long-standing rule against public appearances, his readership is diverse and immense. Increasingly his novels are required reading in literature courses, and the most devoted fans exchange e-mail and debate in chat rooms.[4]

Since much of this study discusses the West as a particular location and somewhat loosely equates it with the frontier, it is prudent to sort out a few historiographical matters. Scholars rely on close definitions and agreed-upon lexicons and, as a result, have spent much time disputing the meaning of certain terms, especially loaded ones such as *frontier* and *the West*. Much effort has been expended trying to establish exactly where the Old West was and when it ended. Frederick Jackson Turner, the first theorist of "the frontier," himself took little time or trouble defining exactly what he meant by the term, offering it as a catchall for both geographical and intellectual spaces. Partly because of this, several generations of historians have taken him to task over his erratic use of the term. Aware of past inconsistencies, most contemporary scholars of the West carefully preface their studies with definitions. Historian Elliot West still finds much value in the concept of "frontier," describing the word as "evocative and elusive" and offering five ways to conceptualize it: as human diversity, an intricate set of power relationships, resources leading to economic opportunities, a region of dynamic transformation, and a locus of symbolic and mythic meanings ("American Frontier" 115–16). As events in the Old West pass beyond history and into legend, we lose sight of their original cultural meanings. The particulars of famous events that occurred a hundred years ago can be as irretrievable as those from the dawn of man. Myth and historical fact soon blend together into popular stories bearing cultural expectations, supporting or challenging our most cherished orthodoxies.

Some historians, such as Patricia Nelson Limerick, have redefined the frontier as a historical "borderland," expanding, changing, moving west as well as north and south. Her paradigm focuses on the cultural exchanges between various ethnic groups sharing the same geographical space ("Borderland" 9). Limerick and others view the migration west as a cultural diaspora in which people arrived in several great migrations, dispossessed of old homelands. The great diversity of Natives, Europeans, African-Americans, Asians, and Latin Americans found themselves sharing the same space in what Elliot West calls a "swapping ground of cultures" ("American Frontier" 137). For various economic, political, and social reasons, they were displaced into a common arena of contested places, often with violent results (Limerick, "Borderland" 8). Many recent studies of this "moveable feast" known as the West explore the cultural transitions and blendings as people sought to adapt familiar customs to a new place.[5]

Allusions to the Old West evoke cultural associations that go beyond their immediate denotations. Barbara Howard Meldrum notes the especially elusive nature of western frontier narrative, calling it a "weighty legacy," since so many writers of the West have confused myth and reality (*Under the Sun* 2). Max Westbrook finds that "problems with national consciousness behind our use of the words *myth* and *reality* are heightened when the subject is the American West" (15). Myths carve deep channels into cultures, especially in the geographical regions of their birth, becoming so familiar they are taken for granted and are thus difficult to map. The term *frontier* retains connotations such as *adventurous, bold, innovative,* and *progressive*. It belongs not only to America's past but to the future: as *Star Trek* reminds us, outer space is the "final frontier." Despite the shock of Vietnam and the subsequent intellectual backlash, the optimistic view of the frontier as part of American exceptionalism seems destined to remain a popular part of mainstream culture. Elliot West concludes that the mystique of the "[frontier] myth has survived, however battered and bent into new shapes" ("Foreword" ix). Limerick acknowledges as well the difficulty of ever eradicating the term. She admits that as a "mental artifact" it continues to be "laden with positive associations" ("Persistence" 24). Walt Whitman perhaps captured the most essential element of the western frontier when he described Custer's Last Stand as heroism in a "fatal environment," reenacting the "old, old legend of our race, / The loftiest of life upheld by death."[6]

Perhaps these mythic connotations of the Old West shouldn't be so surprising. According to Joseph Campbell, the most universal and popular of mythical figures in any culture is the warrior-hero, a figure who willingly sacrifices his life to defend kith and kin. Campbell knows of "no primitive people anywhere that either rejects and despises conflict or represents warfare as an absolute evil" (170). In the American pantheon as well, the frontier hero is undoubtedly the most recognizable. In three definitive studies of the Old West and its influence on American culture, Richard Slotkin provides numerous examples of frontier figures who have embodied various national ideals, including Benjamin Church, Daniel Boone, Cooper's Natty Bumppo, Andrew Jackson, Davy Crockett, Kit Carson, George Armstrong Custer, Jessie James, Wyatt Earp, Buffalo Bill Cody, Teddy Roosevelt, John Wayne, and Clint Eastwood—all characters whose value depends not so much on historical reality as on mythic associations. Literary characters, actors, and politicians in western clothes play upon our collective imagination as much as real cowboys and gunfighters. Slotkin's chief premise is that the traditional American hero engages in "redemptive acts of violence" which promote Anglo-American interests through displacement or destruction of the indigenous tribal cultures. This decidedly xenophobic American hero can be traced back to the early seventeenth-century captivity narratives in which Puritans took the common European myth of the wild man along with their religious conceptions of demons and personified them as Indians.

McCarthy's West is divided between the stark, unforgiving brutality of *Blood Meridian* and the primitive-pastoral visions of the Border Trilogy. It is a surprising change of heart, since authors, like other artists, usually revise the same story, relying on a set of experiences and a philosophical worldview to produce similar themes, characters, and motifs. The publication of *All the Pretty Horses* in 1992 constitutes the beginning of a new period in McCarthy's artistic career that most readers are hard-pressed

INTRODUCTION

to explain. Although his signature prose is still recognizable,[7] the thematic shift away from atavistic violence and iconoclastic characters is astounding. And as McCarthy has never granted interviews (with one exception), he has not publicly discussed this abrupt change in sensibility. But given the best-selling success of the Border Trilogy, the new formula has worked. Finally McCarthy has given people what they want, the stuff of their mythic dreams.

It has been a pleasure scrutinizing McCarthy's novels these past months. I have enjoyed the labyrinth of critical trails among the library stacks, the small discoveries, the textual interconnections, the sudden insights. Like almost everyone else, I am convinced McCarthy's use of the English language is without parallel in contemporary American literature; his distinctive juxtaposition of rough-hewn, barbed vernacular alongside the astonishingly poetic narrative is as recognizable as any great film director's work. McCarthy's technical prowess with words and thematic motifs will ensure his inclusion in college courses for years to come. I first encountered his amazing writing in *Blood Meridian,* which, despite the critical and popular success of the Border Trilogy, I still find the most compelling and profoundly disturbing of his works. It sticks in my gullet, an indigestible enigma. I want to save the kid, to defend the human race. But the novel's obsessive insistence on its theme is too persuasive. Judge Holden's cold, hard logic concerning the affairs of men is too firmly planted in the graveyard of historical bedrock. I find myself thumbing through the pages of *Blood Meridian.* "The mystery is that there is no mystery," states the judge (252). No, that can't be right—it doesn't even make sense. I don't want it to make sense. This study was born from the pangs of such struggle—to do what the kid was never capable of—to answer the judge with words, not just spit.

Cormac McCarthy's Western Novels

One

Blood Meridian's Violence

There's no such thing as life without bloodshed.
—Cormac McCarthy

Although *Blood Meridian* has generated more academic interest than any of McCarthy's other novels, readers are forced to come to terms with its shocking assault, page after page. Rather than leading us into a classical, Aristotelian progression by setting the plot and describing the main characters, normally a slow accretion of details portending the conflict between protagonist and antagonist, to be settled in a climactic denouement, McCarthy plunges us headlong into an unrelenting thematic exposition in which "riding on" only leads to more of the same. It is History 101 with a vengeance. The first sentence of the novel is "See the child" (3), an ironic echo of Alexander Pope's "Behold the child, by Nature's kindly law / Pleased with a rattle, tickled with a straw" (*Essay on Man,* "Epistle II," lines 274–75). McCarthy's is a savage child born with a savage nature in woods that "harbor yet a few last wolves" (3), and his "essay on man" will overturn the Enlightenment's motif of the innocent child and hopes for civilized man. In the world of *Blood Meridian,* Virtue does not defeat Vice. McCarthy's protagonist, known simply as the kid, is introduced as a primal First Man: "He can neither read nor write and in him broods already a taste for mindless violence. All history present in that visage, the child the father of the man" (3). Although the kid's father "has been a schoolmaster," he now "lies in drink" (3). With his mother dead in childbirth and neglected by his father, the kid is "pale and unwashed" (3). When he runs away at fourteen, he is launched into the "Antaean" world. The kid "wanders west" (4), then south to New Orleans, where he is submitted to Darwinian rites of initiation, as he fights each night with drunken sailors: "They fight with fists, with feet, with bottles or knives. All races, all breeds. Men whose speech sounds like the grunting of apes" (4). McCarthy reiterates his thematic point early on: "The child's face is curiously untouched behind the scars, the eyes oddly innocent" (4). The references to "all races, all breeds" and the child's innocence and the ape motif reveal McCarthy's thesis: mindless, atavistic violence is the true nature of mankind, a genetic heritage in common with apes and wolves.

On one of these nights he is shot in the back and "again just below the heart" (4). It is to be the first of many such near-death encounters. After recovering, the kid continues west, encountering a "parricide hanged in a crossroads hamlet," hanging "dead from his rope while urine darkens his trousers" (5). In the next scene, reminiscent of Sam Peckinpah's *The Wild Bunch,* which also begins with a church meeting, we see Judge Holden transforming an itinerant evangelist's tent meeting into chaos: "gunfire was general within the tent and a dozen exits had been hacked through the canvas walls and people were pouring out, women screaming, folk stumbling, folk trampled underfoot in the mud" (7). Many more ruined churches will follow. Throughout the novel, violence overwhelms the tabernacles of Christianity, lending the primal theme an iconoclastic aura. Soon, the kid fights for his life on a muddy boardwalk against the earless Toadvine, who lunges "after him with the jagged bottleneck . . . to stick it in his eye" (9). After recovering from this battle, the kid and Toadvine amicably form an alliance, setting fire to a hotel, murdering a man by kicking him to death. As the kid pauses on his way out of town to look back at their handiwork, the judge smiles approvingly—the first of many such chilling Cheshire cat smiles, which reappears as one of the novel's motifs.

Everywhere the kid travels in this bleak western landscape, there are signs of violence and death. An old "anchorite" shows him a "man's heart, dried and blackened" (18). The next day he passes a "load of corpses" piled into a wagon (22). That night the kid calmly kills a bartender who fails to serve him a drink by smashing a "bottle across the barman's skull and [cramming] the jagged remnant into his eye" (25). The next morning he awakens in a ruined mission that contains "the remains of several bodies, one a child" (26). Soon after, one of his new drinking buddies from Captain White's band is murdered "with his skull broken in a pool of blood, none knew by whom" (40). So goes the carnage. As part of Captain White's filibustering expedition, the kid rides south across the border into Mexico, where four men die from disease (45). The desert is littered with the evidence of death: "They saw half-buried skeletons of mules with the bones so white and polished they seemed incandescent even in that blazing heat and they saw panniers and packsaddles and the bones of men and they saw a mule entire, the dried and blackened carcass hard as iron" (46). The band sleeps "like pilgrims exhausted upon the face of the planet Anareta" (46), which, as Leo Daugherty notes, is an obscure but very apt Renaissance allusion to a "'planet which destroys life'" where "'violent deaths are caused'"(161). At night the very landscape through which "they rode on," to use one of McCarthy's favorite motifs, becomes a surreal nightmare of violent lightning storms: "[They] quaked sourceless to the west beyond the midnight thunderheads, making a bluish day of the distant desert, the mountains on the sudden skyline stark and black and livid . . . like some demon kingdom summoned up" (47).

Two days later the men encounter a large dust cloud, and seeing a few Indians, Captain White anticipates, with an arrogance reminiscent of General Custer, "a little sport" (51). Instead, Comanches appear by the hundreds: "a legion of horribles . . . wardrobed out of a fevered dream with the skins of animals and silk finery and pieces of uniform still tracked with the blood of prior owners, coats of slain dragoons, frogged and braided cavalry jackets, one in a stovepipe hat and one with an umbrella and one in white stockings and a bloodstained weddingveil and some in headgear of cranefeathers or rawhide helmets" (52). They are comic grotesques adorned in parti-colored war paint and assorted booty. Like demonic incarnations of "mounted clowns, death hilarious" (53), they ride down upon the small group of filibusters and slaughter them without mercy. Here McCarthy's minuteness of detail casts us into the agonizing slow motion of dying horses and gutted viscera, and the camera obscura of death unswervingly remains focused. Without respite, our attention is riveted by painful realism in a series of long, gory, Faulknerian sentences:

> Everywhere there were horses down and men scrambling and he saw a man who sat charging his rifle while blood ran from his ears and he saw men with their revolvers disassembled trying to fit the spare loaded cylinders they carried and he saw men kneeling who tilted and clasped their shadows on the ground and he saw men lanced and caught up by the air and scalped standing and he saw the horses of war trample down the fallen and a little whitefaced pony with one clouded eye leaned out of the murk and snapped at him like a dog and was gone. . . . [Warriors were] stripping the clothes from the dead and seizing them up by the hair and passing their blades about the skulls of the living and the dead alike and snatching aloft the bloody wigs and hacking and chopping at the naked bodies, ripping off limbs, heads, gutting the strange white torsos and holding up great handfuls of viscera, genitals, some of the savages so slathered up with gore they might have rolled in it like dogs and some who fell upon the dying and sodomized them with loud cries to their fellows. (53–54)

This shocking scene does not appease us with narrative distance. Without qualms or mincing words, McCarthy has demonstrated the novel's theme. Primal violence is the novel's common denominator, the leitmotif, the horrible adumbration.

Two survivors of the Comanche massacre, the kid and Sproule, soon come across dead babies hung "by their throats from the broken stobs of a mesquite to stare eyeless at the naked sky. Bald and pale and bloated, larval to some unreckonable being" (57). As "witnesses," another of McCarthy's favorite motifs, they stumble into a sacked village, burned and smoking, with all inhabitants slaughtered, some of them in another church full of rotting bodies: "Flies clambered over the peeled and wigless skulls of the dead and flies walked on their shrunken eyeballs" (60–61). Soon afterward Sproule dies from his wounds, and the kid is captured by Mexican soldiers, who take him to Chihuahua. There he sees Captain White's decapitated head in "glass carboy of clear mescal" (69). Like the anchorite's "dried and blackened heart" and Toadvine's string of ears, the head is a primitive trophy of war. Thus ends the first section of *Blood Meridian*. But the killing is just beginning. Next the kid is recruited by the Glanton gang and participates in scalp hunting. The gang soon exceeds its commission of eradicating Apaches for bounty by murdering peaceful Indians and Mexicans as well, since all black scalps, or "receipts," as Glanton calls them, tend to look alike.

All readers of *Blood Meridian* are initially blasted by the pace and the graphic argot of unmitigated, resonating violence. Its pall lingers in our consciousness, hanging like smoke "from the ruins" (57), one scene boding another as the body count climbs with every page. We too witness the novel's crime. While scholars have clashed over McCarthy's thematic intent, they are unanimous in reacting with initial shock and dismay, like the sergeant in Captain White's militia who looks up with dread at the approaching Comanches and mutters, "Oh my god" (53). At some deep level our moral equilibrium has been disturbed, and the author does not pause for comforting reflection to help us regain balance. The text is pure anoesis, sensation without understanding, devoid of ethical or mythic comfort. McCarthy's amoral vision of frontier violence is one of mankind running amok, subverting law at every bend in the trail and rendering all moral questions "void and without warrant" (250). McCarthy's West is indeed a "fatal environment," yet unlike Walt Whitman's it is unheroic. In *Blood Meridian* there is no progressive myth of good overcoming evil, no courageous men taming the West for civilization. Instead, Captain White's militia and Glanton's gang are both examples of man's primal rapacity.

Even the landscape lacks any romance. Unlike the Border Trilogy, *Blood Meridian* is without pathos, pastoralism, or nostalgia. The land itself has been blasted and pitted by eons of natural violence—wind, water, earthquakes, volcanoes—into terrifying, sublime postures: "They crossed the blackened wood of a burn and they rode through a region of cloven rock where great boulders lay halved with smooth uncentered faces and on the slopes of those ferric grounds old paths of fire and the blackened bones of trees assassinated in the mountain storms" (187–88). Man reflects the violent character of a brutal environment. For all of man's improvements and curious wanderlust, he is still apish, ready to kill upon the least provocation.

Critical response has split over the meaning and effect of *Blood Meridian*'s extreme violence. Caryn James states, "*Blood Meridian* comes at the reader like a slap in the face, an affront that asks us to endure a vision of the Old West full of charred human skulls, blood-soaked scalps" and a tree "hung with the bodies of dead infants" (31). She also notes the attraction of McCarthy's poetic language, his "lyricism," which contrasts with the "ugliness" of its images (31). Terrence Morgan sees an "immense amount of slaughter" and surmises that McCarthy might be parodying popular Westerns (37). While praising the novel's descriptions as "evocative passages," he is disturbed by the grotesque scenes of "horrible massacre or sickening degeneracy" (37). Mark Winchell finds *Blood Meridian* "considerably more harrowing" than McCarthy's earlier novels but, like Morgan, sees the excessive violence as a problem because "sustained and senseless violence . . . can shock for only so long before it begins to numb," and concludes that "boredom" sets in (308). Tom Nolan calls the violence "a theological purgative, an allegory on the nature of evil as timeless as Goya's hallucinations on war, monomaniacal in its conception and execution" (B2). Tim Parrish notes that the act of criticism itself pulls us back from the novel and "expiate[s] us from acknowledging the identification we form with [its] bloody imaginings" (25). Vereen M. Bell, the first critic to publish a book-length study on McCarthy's novels, admits, "It is not a story for the squeamish, least of all for the philosophically squeamish" (*Achievement* 119). Jonathan Pitts sees the "problem of seeing and killing" as "the novel's thematic heart" (11) and concludes, "It is difficult not to see *Blood Meridian* as nihilistic" (23). Patrick W. Shaw finds correspondences in Eric Fromm's analysis of "'malignant aggression,'" which is "'rooted in the very conditions of human existence,'" to the "phenomenal violence that governs *Blood Meridian*" (Shaw 103–4).

The novel's violence repulses yet attracts. The unrelenting montage of massacre offends our sensibilities. In *The End of History and the Last Man,* Francis Fukuyama discusses this kind of response as a philosophical ambivalence between "desire and reason" (164). Driven by base impulses, such as lust and greed, we aggressively seek to satisfy desires by achieving higher social status and increasing control over others' territory. Fukuyama argues that only the logic of restraint keeps us from engaging in all-out warfare. A consensus to abide by laws that ensure our safety and provide for personal achievement contains a Girardian chaos of selfish, predatory violence. Paradoxically, despite our consensus to obey the law, most of us still desire to witness lawless acts of violence. Fukuyama offers the example of Socrates' story about Leontius, who "wants to look at a pile of corpses lying by the public executioner" (164): "He desired to look, but at the same time he was disgusted and made himself turn away; and for a while he struggled and covered his face. But finally, overpowered by the desire, he opened his eyes wide, ran toward the corpses and said: 'Look, you damned wretches, take your fill of the fair sight'" (164). New York author Peter Josyph, encountering all manner of real violence on the streets, wrestles with his mixed feelings about the fictional violence in *Blood Meridian*:

> McCarthy's appetite for characters who lean toward the brute, the bloody, the brawlerous, the chronically monosyllabic, the psycho- and socio-pathic, is a literary propensity the reader need not share in order to marvel at the important talent at work.... But when a highly charged, richly textured novel driven by some of the most impressive American prose of this century features no major figure who is not, quite literally, a slaughterer, and offers scarcely a single act to inspire hope for the race, it is natural to ask questions about that talent and to wonder whether one is perceiving it rightly and judging it fairly. One gluts upon a baroque of thieving, raping, shooting, slashing, hanging, scalping, burning, bashing, hacking, stabbing ... (170)

This strong reaction leads Josyph to read the novel again, but this time "every word of it, aloud" (170) to find some answers. Although his initial enjoyment of the novel's beautiful, poetic prose is validated upon second reading, his problems with the apparent amorality of the characters remain unresolved. His friend, noted surgeon and author Richard Selzer, while "knocked flat by the range of language, imagery—the richness, the mastery of lore" is also dumbfounded and deeply disturbed. He writes to Josyph that his "one trouble" was that "the violence is there for its own sake.... He is a genius—also probably somewhat insane" (Josyph 176).

The intensity of *Blood Meridian* provokes all readers to ask, "Why?"

Since McCarthy is famously reticent about giving interviews or discussing his work in public, we must answer this question ourselves. Critics and reviewers have offered several possibilities:

1. The novel embodies contemporary historical revisionism and its moral indictment of European conquest as it developed in the West.
2. McCarthy isn't as good a writer as his prose first indicates.
3. McCarthy is a mad genius with a fetish for sensational violence.

My own study of this novel pursues other interpretations. First, McCarthy draws on contemporary images of violence from the news media and popular films, and while *Blood Meridian* is indeed part of the continuing reassessment of violence in American culture, it is not a political ally of the revisionist movement. Second, the novel is grounded thematically in turn-of-the-century naturalism. And third, McCarthy effectively employs several literary elements, including surrealism, bilingualism, doubling, and didacticism to challenge readers to participate in the shocking exploration of man's atavistic nature.

Two general critical camps of scholars responding to the violence have emerged in the last few years: those who agree with parts of Vereen Bell's "nihilist" thesis and those who side with Edwin T. Arnold's defense of McCarthy as a moralist. Most of the saber-rattling began with Vereen Bell's *The Achievement of Cormac McCarthy* (1988). Bell writes that the novels demonstrate a "prevailing gothic and nihilistic mood" (1) and a "perverse and tantalizing density" (2), and that "the motivation of the characters is usually tantalizingly obscure" (4) and "meaning does not prevail over narrative and texture" (5). In "The Ambiguous Nihilism of Cormac McCarthy," Bell offers an even stronger critique of the author's skills, adding that the novels "are as innocent of theme and of ethical reference as they are of plot" (31). Like other readers, however, Bell does not fault the prose, and even transforms his negative criticism into a sort of backhanded praise by arguing that McCarthy's lack of plot and characterization enables him to create "a densely created world as authentic and persuasive as any that there is in fiction" (31).

Edwin T. Arnold has led the charge in defense of McCarthy. He asserts that the novels do contain "moral parables" and "a profound belief in the need for moral order, a conviction that is essentially religious" (Arnold and Luce 44), along with many religious references. Arnold maintains that McCarthy's characters are "clearly motivated by those emotions we all share—love, loneliness, guilt, shame, hope, [and] despair." He emphasizes that the kid in *Blood Meridian* finally outgrows his "taste for 'mindless violence'" (62) and concludes that even though he dies without confronting the judge's view of humanity, the "moral choice remains: the judge can still be faced" (63). Most critics of McCarthy do gravitate toward defensive positions, presuming a priori that such an accomplished writer must have a moral theme. In an unpublished dissertation, William C. Spencer, a self-identified student of the anti-Bell school, observes that "at least part of the debate seems to be a problem of semantics" (25), since Bell and his followers also find themes and structures in McCarthy's work. However, Spencer correctly identifies the crux of the debate as a litmus test of whether the "pervasive shocking nature of McCarthy's fiction is gratuitous or justified" (17).

Some elaborate paradigms have been entered as evidence of the novel's underlying morality. Leo Daugherty presents *Blood Meridian* as a gnostic Greek tragedy, with the kid playing the role of tragic hero. Daugherty's analysis is compelling while he discusses the history of gnostic cults but encounters serious problems when he maintains that the novel distinguishes between good and evil, with the kid as the good protagonist and the judge as the evil antagonist. According to this scenario, the kid possesses some remnant of the original "spark of alien divine" in our evil world, ruled by archons (158). Daugherty believes the kid's lack of conscious moral development is due to a retarding physical sheath of matter, his corporal body, which is influenced by evil archons. In siding with Arnold's camp, he pointedly gestures toward Bell when he remarks that "gnosticism is easily confused with nihilism" (159). The gnostic thesis works best when placed alongside McCarthy's vivid descriptions of the earth as a primal killing ground with the judge as its archon, or an avenging god of destruction. Less convincing is the premise of the kid as a "tragic hero," which Daugherty himself admits is arguable. He too easily sidesteps this problem, however, in proposing a looser definition of tragedy: "some tragic heroes do not really fill any formulaic bill . . . all that's needed is a dumb kid possessed of a spark of the divine who's outside the will of some Yahweh" (169). Intriguing as Daugherty's reading is, his attempt to define *Blood Meridian* as Greek tragedy fails on two counts: first, because it diverts attention away from the grand theme of primal violence, and second, because he exaggerates the kid's supposed spark of goodness.

Critical attempts to explain away the violence of *Blood Meridian* begin to appear apologetic, or as Lewis Carroll's Alice once mused, "Curiouser and curiouser." Some pro-McCarthy critics accuse Bell of being an anticritic who avoids the kind of careful analysis that would reveal McCarthy's characters in a more favorable light. To my sensibilities, however, Arnold's extreme faith in McCarthy as a creator of moral parables seems far-fetched and overstated, more of a reaction to perceived animadversion than clearheaded analysis. McCarthy himself has unswervingly directed our attention toward "mindless violence" throughout the text, and undue critical attempts to deflect it elsewhere—to tease out the kid's tenuous acts of "clemency," or to dwell on the judge's mysterious character—may very well cloud the initial and recurring shock of witnessing man's atavistic nature. To twist *Blood Meridian* away from its evident purpose doesn't make much sense. To any first-time reader of the novel, violence is obviously the overwhelming visual motif, the principal structural element, and the continuing subject of the judge's sermons. As such, readers appalled by the novel are correctly reacting according to McCarthy's original intent. He is thrusting violence—mindless, amoral, and primal—at us with a graceful but murderous lunge. And the tale he has to tell deserves our attention. We must face it head-on and deal with, in Judge Holden's words, "the bones of things" (116).

Peter Josyph finally condemns McCarthy for juxtaposing violence and comedy. One incident in particular illustrates Josyph's reservations about enjoying the novel too wholeheartedly. When Jackson, a black member of the gang, unhesitatingly kills Owens, the owner of a frontier restaurant, over the latter's refusal to serve a nonwhite, another gang member comments, "Most terrible nigger I have ever seen. . . . Find some plates, Charlie" (236). What disturbs Josyph so much is the lack of moral consequences and the fact that McCarthy uses the violence for a casual, dismissive comic moment that understates the horror. By laughing, we participate in the violence of how "Owens's brains went out the back of his skull and plopped in the floor behind him" (236). Josyph finds such moments of admiring "the quick over the dead" to be "ethically bereft," containing a "sneering kind of bravado" (185). The prevalence of laughter alongside violence finally leads Josyph to complain of the work's "emotional stinginess, a kind of aridity, at its core" (186). In his ambivalence, Josyph misses McCarthy's theme. Black Jackson's swift executions of his racist double, White Jackson, and later of Owens are provoked by their intolerance of his race. McCarthy's point is that integration is most effectively achieved through the low court of survival of the fittest. When a white man acts with prejudice, Black Jackson's justice is swift and extreme. No further arguments or appeals are required.

But McCarthy's humor does warrant more attention. It is indeed difficult to laugh when our moral sensibilities are being so thoroughly challenged. Wade Hall interprets the humor merely as part of the intended realism: "Any writer who attempts to portray life honestly and unvarnished will write comedy" ("Human Comedy" 49). The problem with this kind of comic realism is that it gets uncomfortably close, and the laughter becomes macabre, full of dark ironies. Hall wryly notes that the novel's "final truth is horror" and that "life's epitaph, the last sound of any self-aware person, is demonic laughter" (50). Rick Wallach finds that "much of McCarthy's humor derives from the folkways and folkspeech of his uniliterate characters" (Hall, "Human Comedy" 56). The vernacular diction of his characters is ungrammatical enough to induce laughter. Examples of their comic laconism are found everywhere on the trail. When the kid encounters some men, they tell him about two others who have pulled out:

> Them boys was with us fell in with a bunch from Arkansas. They was headed down for Bexar. Goin to pull for Mexico and the west.
> I bet them old boys is in Bexar drinkin they brains out.
> I'll bet old Lonnie's done topped ever whore in town. (*Blood Meridian* 21)

This passage is typically inane and uneventful except for the chuckles coming in the vernacular comments about drinking and whoring. Like so many of McCarthy's characters, these men pause to exchange small talk. Many critics have noted their literary antecedents in the frontier realism of Mark Twain. The minimal dialogue also owes much to Hemingway's style in its simply constructed syntax and customary western diction. As part of the code of the West, strong men prefer direct action over excessive speech, and quick judgment and skill are valued far above eloquence. As in Teddy Roosevelt's famous adage, "Speak softly and carry a big stick," western men tend to say less than they mean. Too many words might reveal more than a man wants to communicate, such as uncomfortable emotions and insecurities. McCarthy's use of understated western vernacular, like that of his contemporaries Sam Shepard and Larry McMurtry, reflects frontier speech rhythms.

Much of the jocularity is historically accurate and thus offends contemporary taste. Early on, the kid stays a night with an old ex-slaver hermit, who seems friendly enough until he produces a dried human heart and abruptly announces: "They is four things that can destroy the earth, he said. Women, whiskey, money, and niggers" (18). And the callous joke that follows about the cost of the heart is no better:

> That thing costed me two hundred dollars, he said.
> You give two hundred dollars for it?
> I did, for that was the price they put on the black son of a bitch it hung inside of. (18)

McCarthy's macabre sense of humor offends the reader, paradoxically attracting while repulsing. Like the judge, McCarthy's prose smiles at death and laughs at its own horrible truths. Readers are given no clues whether to reject or identify with the characters.

Philosopher Henri Bergson analyzed laughter as a common human reaction to the sudden shock of witnessing something recognizable but somehow different, a phenomenon that Bergson labels "mechanical inelasticity" (10). In such situations, if we cannot quickly label an experience, it becomes incomprehensible. Perceiving a recognizable yet somehow different object creates an uncomfortable tension, a disunity with known experience, which is often accompanied by the laughter reflex. As Bergson notes, a person falling down on ice is funny only because most of the time people do not fall. Another reaction to sudden phenomena, indicating more apprehension, is the panic reflex. While laughter and fear are closely related psychological reactions, fear leads to the famous fight-or-flight response, whereas laughter relieves tension. A sudden stimulus can cause either laughter or fear, depending on the degree of surprise and the perceived danger. A startling event such as an owl hooting loudly at night might produce momentary fear followed by laughter as we realize there is no danger. Much of *Blood Meridian*'s traumatic violence and shocking imagery pushes past the boundaries of conventional fiction and thus produces uncomfortable moments of laughter tinged with fear. Many scenes in the novel may be considered as comic-horror, full of dark satire and gut-wrenching surprises.

Another humorous yet indecorous moment occurs in Tobin's anecdote of Judge Holden's impromptu gunpowder recipe. With menacing Indians chasing just behind, the gang encounters the judge, who is strangely nonchalant at being discovered alone in the middle of nowhere. The judge leads them on a wild climb to the rim of a volcano, where he mixes sulfur, charcoal, and bat guano together in a "devil's batter" (132). Only one key ingredient is missing:

> We were half mad anyways. All lined up. Delawares and all. Every man save Glanton and he was a study. We hauled forth our members and at it we went and the judge on his knees kneadin the mass with his naked arms and the piss was splashin about and he was cryin out to us to piss, man, piss for your very souls for cant you see the redskins yonder, and laughin the while and workin up this great mass in a foul black dough, a devil's batter by the stink of it and him not a bloody dark pastryman himself I don't suppose. . . . (132)

The vignette serves several purposes: first, as a rousing adventure yarn in the Old West tradition of the tall tale, with good cowboys conventionally pitted against bad Indians; and second, as an introduction to the Faustian bargain between the judge and Glanton's gang. The story often refers to Judge Holden's charismatic power over the gang, as if they are his "disciples of a new faith" (130). The first time Glanton's gang encounters him, the judge appears phantomlike on the rock, alone without a canteen, "smilin as we rode up. Like he'd been expectin us" (125). Glanton soon forms a "secret commerce. Some terrible covenant" (126), which leads to the miraculous science of Holden's gunpowder saving the day, deus ex machina.

Like Josyph, many of us are disturbed by laughter juxtaposed with gore. The yo-yo effect is emotionally disconcerting and confounds easy pigeonholing. We want to label experience, to laugh or fight or take flight. But in this novel, conventional catchalls and caveats fail. Is McCarthy spinning an adventure story, a tall tale, tragedy, horror, historical romance, dark comedy, revisionist fiction, or some kind of postmodern experiment? McCarthy refuses to allow us any easy answers. As we continue reading page after page of violence and unsettling jokes, we make our own Faustian bargain with the novel, a secret commerce of laughing and queasy participation. The judge's strange philosophy intrigues us. But the violence is too real, too intense for us to recover our equilibrium. Patricia Nelson Limerick summarizes our paradoxical desire to experience the myth of the Old West without looking too closely:

> [Our] image of the frontier balances precariously between too much reality and too little. . . . Properly screened and edited, the doings of the Old Frontier are quite a bit of fun. But when encounters with death, or injury, or conflict, or loss become unexpectedly convincing and compelling, then fun can make an abrupt departure, while emotions considerably more troubling take its place. ("Adventures of the Frontier" 69)

Perhaps the reader's wry laughter is a subconscious reaction to resist the novel's evil, as one would "resist the devil" (James 4.7). After all, the judge is always found smiling when nobody knows the joke. The first time the judge sees the kid leaving town, he smiles (14), and again in Chihuahua (79) and again at Black Jackson during the uncomfortable foreboding of the tarot cards, telling him with malicious glibness to "Beware the demon rum" (93). In Fort Griffin's bar near the end, he smiles with "great teeth" bared (329). John Sepich, who has counted thirty-eight instances of the judge smiling in the novel, calls his smile an "enigma" (160). It disturbs because the judge represents an ultimate purveyor of violence, a devil and a man, an Antaean set of juxtaposed opposites: childlike yet giant, perverse yet wise, barbaric yet cultured, murderous yet kind. His smile charms yet deceives; it is a smug, Cheshire cat smile of preternatural knowledge and unlimited powers. The judge's cunning is displayed early on, after he breaks up Reverend Green's tent meeting by alleging that Green had committed "congress with a goat" at Fort Smith. But later Holden abruptly admits to the men in a bar, "I was never in Fort Smith in my life. Doubt that he was" and "I never laid eyes on the man before today. Never even heard of him" (8). The men react to this bizarre confession first with a confused silence "like mud effigies" and then by breaking out in sudden laughter (8). The affair seems to be one of the judge's little pranks, but his power of manipulation is absolute. The judge, like an Old Testament prophet, speaks of mysteries, as during the reading of tarot cards, when he offers encrypted details foretelling the gang members' deaths. Rick Wallach calls the judge's frustrating yet compelling rhetoric "deliberate obfuscation" and quotes Frank Kermode's view that the novel may "'proclaim a truth like a herald, and at the same time conceal truth like an oracle'" (131–32). His smile—along with the smiles of bats, lizards, and corpses—is the leering pantomime of "death hilarious" (53). At the end of the novel, the judge, naked and immense in his "terrible flesh," smiles one last time as the kid steps into the jakes (333). It is enough to make one take up frowning.

While much of the ongoing debate between Bell's "nihilism" and Arnold's "moral parable" may sound more like a shibboleth than a real issue, it does get at the problem of *Blood Meridian*'s violence. Critics who insist on finding intellectual solace in arcane interpretations are most likely finding their "heart's desire" (252) rather than struggling with the amorality of McCarthy's "godless charivari" (190). This may be one literary bone we should all choke on. It is too easy to assert that McCarthy is simply recreating historical events, as Sepich maintains, for the "comparison of traditional versions of an event with the author's personalized version" (2). But this is not a historical novel akin to Michael Sheridan's *Killer Angels,* which recounts painstakingly researched details for the delight of history buffs. An appeal to historical validity does not satisfy our deeper horror in the here and now about the awful fictional rendering of historical violence. *Blood Meridian* should not be reduced to the historical romance described by Sepich, who imagines that the "'people of that time' would have found [its] people and places 'probable' to the extent that the novel might have been written for them" (2). Sepich himself initially calls the novel "three hundred pages of grotesque evidence" (1). Any reader before our own post-Vietnam era would have been, if anything, even more shocked by the preponderance of the novel's graphic violence. McCarthy's original historical sources, such as Sam Chamberlain's *My Confession* (discussed admirably at length in Sepich's *Notes*), do not dare portray real events so graphically. *Blood Meridian* must be seen as more than a clever historical reenactment, by virtue of its style, its extreme depiction, and its resistance to conventional mythos. And despite what some critics have said, the novel is not artistically flawed or the product of an insane genius. Its extreme violence is deliberately paced to dramatically overwhelm and subsume all other structural elements. The judge, for all his bellicose grandiosity, constantly and patiently preaches to us about the primal nature of mankind, although the gang members, like the original disciples, seem unable to comprehend the sermon. But we cannot share their fate. We must explore "what manner of thing we have here" (133); we must unfold McCarthy's parables of violence, however horrifying they may be.

Two

Blood Meridian and the Reassessment of Violence

It is suggested that society is too difficult to understand and history impossible to predict.—Norman Mailer (1959)

It's quite unpleasant to think that a country with a noble dream... could possibly continue to initiate, participate, and then continue in a war of this unimaginable horror.
—Congressman Phillip Burton in the *Dellums Committee Hearings on War Crimes in Vietnam*

In 1959, as America enjoyed its great shining moment as the world's most powerful nation, no one could foresee the enormous cultural stresses of the next decade. Despite the Korean War and the escalating Cold War, most Americans, including many historians and writers, waved the brave flags of consensus ideology. But so often, as Judge Holden foretells in *Blood Meridian*, "... in the affairs of men there is no waning and the noon of his expression signals the onset of night. His spirit is exhausted at the peak of its achievement" (146–47). Today, many Americans admit that our nationalism has historically been self-serving and imperialistic, moving west and north and south along with the frontier, then leapfrogging whole oceans, to Hawaii, the Philippines, Korea, and Vietnam. But the reassessment of American history as brutal conquest has been clearly promulgated only in the last thirty years. Until the mid-sixties, most Americans—including historians, authors, and filmmakers—believed unquestioningly in the western myth of progress. Patriotism masked the old rifts of segregation and hegemonic control by white males. The intoxicating mix of economic, industrial, and military might was another strain of nationalism about to run amok. For this American generation was to witness, on TV every night, a plummet over the precipice into the abyss of the Vietnam War and the resulting war in the streets at home. The shocking horror of this spectacle—the firefights, body counts, riots, fires, tear gas, high-pressure hoses—proved to be America's bloody meridian, the "darkening and the evening of [our] day" (147).

A brief review of the violence of the Vietnam era will place *Blood Meridian* more clearly in its social context. The official search-and-destroy tactics of our troops in Vietnam, especially in free-fire zones, regressed into primal violence as bands of loosely disciplined men took the war into their own hands. As became apparent after the revelation of the My Lai massacre in 1969, at the trial of Lieutenant William Calley, and later in the ad hoc congressional hearings conducted by Representative Ronald Dellums in 1971, American soldiers routinely tortured, killed, and maimed not only Vietcong but also innocent villagers. A Girardian firestorm of violence spread from the battlefields to the streets of America as the fight for civil rights and antiwar protests ignited unstoppable crown fires.[1] The conflagration overseas and at home resulted in a chaotic decade, at a time when mass media were publishing and broadcasting unprecedented images of violence in magazines and on TV. As one of the most violent novels in contemporary American literature, *Blood Meridian* parallels its times. The mirror of art that McCarthy holds up to the nineteenth century reflects the ugliness of our own time as well.

Most writers engage various aspects of their culture, taking sides in ongoing debates, questioning authority, rejecting certain parts of the whole. Yet this dialectic process usually remains firmly within the context of a particular set of ideologies, narrative structures, and cultural images that provide the necessary constellations of their experience. Thus the great discussions of any generation rarely move beyond the collective experiences of its participants. Writers usually tell the stories they know best: from childhood experiences, specific geographical regions, ethnicities, and cultural norms. Great works of art are largely molded by the era they are produced in. As Sam Shepard once remarked, "Imagination is great, as far as it will get you. But it usually doesn't get you any farther than your own experience." Within any cultural debate is the implicit agreement to address the topics at hand. To completely escape the gravity of one's culture is to be lost in the void of meaningless space. We cannot examine the extreme violence of *Blood Meridian* without examining the violence of its cultural birth.

Richard Slotkin argues that frontier myths have driven American ideology, from the first settlers on, as the rationale for ignoring our brutal conquest of Native peoples. By citing examples from history, literature, and film, Slotkin demonstrates how America persistently reformulates contemporary frontier heroes into national icons who fight for progress and "redemption through violence."[2] Traditional western romances served as ritualized mythic narratives for a people who lusted after new lands with all the fever of Manifest Destiny. There was much at stake, a literal bonanza of opportunities—in furs, gold, silver, in ranching and farming, new towns and businesses. Frontier communities rose and fell like new stocks, some booming, others busting while a full-blown diaspora of immigrants and speculators rushed in. The violent consequences of this land-grabbing had to be rationalized and then incorporated into the national mythos. A persuasive sense of mission—predicated on the superiority of the dominant Anglo-Saxon culture and Christianity—had to be firmly planted in the popular imagination. Like the British, with their "white man's burden," Americans founded colonies in the West, subdued the natives, and spread Christianity.

To uncover the cultural impetus of *Blood Meridian,* we must examine some ramifications of this century's most unpopular American war, the Vietnam conflict. Like the War with Mexico and the Philippines Conflict, Vietnam spawned a counterculture of war protesters. During the Vietnam era the "peaceniks" joined the already well-organized civil rights movement and for a while garnered national attention by directing a popular hue and cry against the prevailing myth of American progress. Eventually, after the war and the passage of new laws, the two movements dissipated in various ways out into the more conservative mainstream. Two lasting effects of this era can be traced in the emergence of historical revisionism and the escalation of violence in American film and literature.

President Kennedy drew on the old frontier myth to inspire a "New Frontier" in American policy, including space exploration and the war against Communism. Responding to demands that Americans should leave Vietnam, President Johnson once quipped, "There was no back door at the Alamo" (Faragher et al. 930). But as the war dragged on and casualties mounted, such answers did not satisfy many Americans. By 1967, the be-ins and teach-ins and other demonstrations were less about the Summer of Love than the alarming escalation of war overseas (930). Forces had been coalescing on the Berkeley campus since 1964 with the Free Speech Movement, which had long advocated civil rights. But the peace movement and the nonviolence of Martin Luther King turned violent in 1967, when major riots broke out in many cities, including San Francisco, Milwaukee, Dayton, Cleveland, Newark, and Detroit. *Time* magazine called it "the scene of the bloodiest uprising in a half century and the costliest . . . in U.S. history" (see Faragher et al. 937).

And the events of 1968 boded no better, as hopes for peace, at home and abroad, were crushed by a series of crises. Never before had such violence been depicted so openly in the mass media. Newspapers, magazines, television, and films were full of images of carnage. In January of that year the Tet Offensive, mounted by the Vietcong troops, surprised and overran American forces throughout South Vietnam. Americans increasingly lost confidence that the rice paddies of a distant land mattered. Neither setting nor ideology was convincing. It wasn't so much the disproof of the military's claim that the occupied cities were impregnable from Vietcong attacks, or the strained efforts to reassure by politicians and generals. No, it was the firefights on TV, with panicked reporters broadcasting live in the middle of gunfire and mortars. The official rhetoric of necessary intervention, the distancing, abstract metaphor of nations lined up like political dominoes, was overwhelmed every night by the terrifying sounds and pictures of war. Stanley Karnow, a longtime war correspondent and author of the best-selling history of Vietnam, describes one of the most shocking events filmed in Saigon during the Tet Offensive, when South Vietnamese General Nguyen Ngoc Loan, chief of the national police force, interrogated a suspected Vietcong:

> The soldiers marched him up to Loan, who drew his revolver and waved the bystanders away. Without hesitation, Loan stretched out his right arm, placed the short snout of the weapon against the prisoner's head, and squeezed the trigger. The man grimaced—then, almost in slow motion, his legs crumpled beneath him as he seemed to sit down backward, blood gushing from his head as it hit the pavement. Not a word was spoken. It all happened instantly, with hardly a sound except for the crack of Loan's gun, the click of Adams's shutter, and the whir of Vo Suu's camera. (Karnow 529)

The next day this image was printed on the front pages of American newspapers, and "NBC broadcast its exclusive film of the event" (529). Robert Stone identifies the Tet Offensive as the defining moment for the news media, since they were, for the first time, on the front lines without the veil of military censorship. "With Tet, Vietnam finally got America's attention. Millions of Americans watched the battle for Saigon on the evening news, and many who were not personally involved took notice for the first time. In the winter dusk of America as 1968 proceeded, dreadful sights were broadcast. The cameras recorded burnings, executions, even the sight of American soldiers falling in battle" (Stone and Fischer 108).

Militarily, the Tet Offensive may have been only a minor setback, as tense officials at home kept explaining, but most Americans were finally aware that the war was not going to be won easily and that casualties would be high. Tet alone left sixteen hundred dead and eight thousand wounded Americans in three weeks, with reports estimating hundreds of thousands of Vietnamese casualties and over one million refugees. Suddenly half of Americans polled indicated that the war was a mistake, and television commentators, including the paternal Walter Cronkite, urged politicians to negotiate for peace (Faragher et al. 939). But chaotic forces, a Pandora's box of violence, were being unleashed. In the years to follow, violence at home would reach an apogee not seen since the Civil War (939). President Nixon, elected in 1968 and 1972 on promises to stop the war, actually escalated our involvement by bombing Hanoi and invading Laos and Cambodia.

Many scenes in *Blood Meridian* have an eerie resonance for a Vietnam-era audience. General Loan's street execution is the ghostly cultural double behind the shocking scene of Glanton's casual execution of the old Indian woman in a Mexican village (*Blood Meridian* 98). Glanton's ruthlessness is underscored by his cool demeanor as he examines the "receipt" (98) in "the way a man might qualify the pelt of an animal" (99). Another unforgettable image is the scapular of heathen ears, which Toadvine, an earless man, ironically wears as a primitive war trophy. The grisly string of ears passes like an amulet of bad luck from Toadvine to Brown to a soldier, and finally to the kid after Brown is hung. And we still find the kid (who is relabeled "the man") wearing them twenty-nine years later on the trail to Fort Griffin. The string of ears is a primitive tribal signifier, an atavistic reminder of violent death and the kid's lawless period with the Glanton gang. Along the trail to Fort Griffin, it causes a dispute between "the man" and a younger double, which turns lethal later in the night (321). The ears are a literal string of "witnesses" attesting to frontier killing—a badge of merit earned by participation in primal violence. Readers may well recall similar war trophies taken by American soldiers, as documented by numerous veterans returning with war stories. In *The Things They Carried,* Vietnam War veteran Tim O'Brien describes one of the soldiers, "otherwise a very gentle person," who carried a thumb, hacked off "a VC corpse, a boy of fifteen or sixteen" (13). Charles Stephens, of the 101st Airborne Division, remembers how it became an unspoken battalion standard operating procedure, or SOP, to cut the right ear off everybody they killed "to prove our body count" (qtd. in *Winter Soldier* 9). Scott Camil, of the 1st Marine Division, describes the "cutting off of ears, cutting off of heads, torturing of prisoners" that occurred in his company, and admits: "People cut off ears, and when they'd come back in off of an operation you'd make deals before you'd go out and like for every ear you cut off someone would buy you two beers, so people cut off ears" (12–13). Frank Shepard, of the 9th Infantry Division, remembers that his battalion awarded badges for confirmed Vietcong kills, and that one "common way" was "to cut off the ear of the dead Vietnamese and bring it in" (56). As a helicopter pilot in Vietnam, Glen McCoy mentions the "sight of human scalps and ears worn on the belts of the special forces" (McCoy 57). More than any story or scar, the ears, like scalps, are visible proof of success in war, announcing graphically, without words, *I am alive, and the owners of these are dead*. Tim O'Brien states this most succinctly in "How to Tell a True War Story": "You can tell a true war story by its absolute and uncompromising allegiance to obscenity and evil" (*Things They Carried* 76).

In popular wars, America's military defeats have been quickly reformulated into national sacrifices, part of the framework of mythic progress, and are usually followed by a popular call to arms: "Remember the Alamo," Buffalo Bill's "First Scalp for Custer," and Pearl Harbor's aftermath. But no such calls rang forth during Vietnam. Instead, antiwar forces at home organized protests, throwing both real and ideological rocks at American authorities, calling police "pigs" and soldiers "baby killers." In the revised frontier myth, the Indians became good and the cowboys bad, while progress and its accompanying technology were evil, full of military, chemical, and nuclear hazards. War was no longer to be considered as a Clausewitzian "continuation of politics by other means." No, the new term was simpler and more direct: *genocide*. This was the true description of western conquest, which was the story of superior firepower, the proof of Mao's saying that political power grows out of "the barrel of a gun."

In the age of television, the images of protest and war spoke to the nation more clearly and forcefully than the hollow-sounding official press releases:

> Two sets of images, conveyed in print and television photography, symbolized the undoing of these paired strategies [the War on Poverty and the war in Vietnam]. The first showed armored vehicles and paratroopers drawn from divisions fighting in Vietnam battling with Black rioters in the burning streets of Detroit in July 1967. The second showed American and ARNV soldiers fighting desperately to defend the core installations of regions that were supposedly secure, including the American embassy in Saigon, and then turning their artillery and bombs against the very cities they had been defending in order to recapture them (at heavy cost) from the enemy. The absurd inversion to which the logic of our policies had brought us was inadvertently rendered as a slogan by the American officer

who explained the army's evacuation and destruction of the town of Ben Tre by saying, "We had to destroy Ben Tre in order to save it." (Slotkin, *Gunfighter Nation* 535)

The war abroad looked like the war at home. In 1968 the assassinations of Dr. Martin Luther King, Jr., and Robert Kennedy, and the "police riot" at the Democratic National Convention in Chicago, paralleled the Tet Offensive as the year's most unforgettable images of carnage. TV coverage of pitched battles in Vietnam and photographs of the dead mirrored images of U.S. riots, bombings, and assassinations to make indelible impressions. In 1969, after the battle nicknamed "Hamburger Hill," *Life* magazine "published photographs of the two hundred and forty-two young Americans slain in a single week" (Karnow 601). At times, the body count was running more than eight hundred a month. America's military response was to frantically increase the ratio of bombs dropped and villages attacked to raise the total number of enemy killed, even if it put South Vietnam's civilian population at risk. Meanwhile, in a desperate attempt to stymie criticism, leaders like General William Westmoreland were keeping the real casualty figures secret, feeding the public lower numbers. By 1969 the search-and-destroy tactics employed in Vietnam were clearly out of control when the My Lai massacre became public knowledge: "More than any other single event, the revelation transformed the terms of the ideological and political debate on the war, lending authority to the idea that American society was in the grip of a '"madness"'" (Slotkin, *Gunfighter Nation* 581). "After My Lai," Slotkin writes, "the logic of the captivity/rescue myth required us to identify ourselves as the Indians" (588). My Lai made Americans see Vietnam as the foreign quagmire we would drown in. Instead of orderly troops acting in well-defined, professional operations, our military forces in Vietnam had apparently devolved into bands of soldiers randomly roaming the countryside, burning, raping, and pillaging. Reports of carpet bombing, napalm, torture and free-fire zones shocked not only the radicals but conservative mainstream Americans as well. What were we doing? How was it possible for well-trained American troops, many of them still boys, to be involved in this kind of savage violence? On both sides, losses were horrendous, but the loss of Vietnamese lives was almost unfathomable.

Following the war, various estimates put the total number of Vietnamese casualties at between two and four million (Karnow 11).

Nixon's escalation of the war into Laos and Cambodia, along with the Kent State killings, provoked further protests against American involvement. Once again the parallel was undeniable: violence overseas had prompted violence at home. After Kent State, "More than four hundred universities and colleges shut down as students and professors staged strikes, and nearly a hundred thousand demonstrators marched on Washington" (Karnow 611–12). The widely published scenes of soldiers firing on students looked too much like the newsreels of soldiers in Vietnam. On many campuses, the threat of a police state hung heavy on professors and students. It seemed as if the nation's conservative and liberal forces were increasingly polarized, with liberals accusing conservatives of being aligned with the army, conservatives accusing the liberals of being communists, and both claiming to be victims of unprovoked violence. As Americans watched the body bags and death tolls on TV, the absurdity of the frontier myth became more apparent. A whole era of popular westerns seemed as suddenly outdated as black-and-white film. The John Ford westerns, most of them starring a pro-Vietnam John Wayne, were at odds with the emerging culture. The debunked formula had to be quickly reinvented, and several possibilities presented themselves. Some westerns became comedies, such as TV's *F-Troop* and the films *Support Your Local Sheriff* and *Support Your Local Gunfighter,* starring ever-affable James Garner. Others took on more revisionist aspects—*Little Big Man, Tell Them Willie Boy Is Here, Soldier Blue, McCabe and Mrs. Miller,* and *Buffalo Bill and the Indians*—while *Buck and the Preacher* and *A Man Called Horse* emphasized racial diversity.

Critic Mark Winchell compares McCarthy's work to a Sam Peckinpah film in its shocking manner of fleshing out "gut-bucket nihilism" so rudely placed before an uncomfortable viewer (307) and regards *Blood Meridian* as "a novelization of Peckinpah's West" (308). Peckinpah, a ten-year veteran writer and director of the TV westerns *Gunsmoke* and *The Rifleman,* had already devised a new method of using several cameras filming at different speeds with numerous setups at different angles, and he was notorious for filming as many as forty or fifty takes with major changes in setups. In the editing room, with hours of film to select from, a five-minute battle could be orchestrated and fine-tuned to perfection. By cutting back and forth from a man falling from a building to close-ups of battle, he dramatically increased an audience's sensation of witnessing the impact of bullets passing through bodies, complete with shreds of wet flesh and realistic sounds of bullets ripping through bone. The varying film speeds, quick cuts, and odd angles created a bizarre kind of montage, an American take on the European *cinema vérité*, a technique that captured the dizzy violence of a firefight so effectively that some people couldn't sit through his films. Perhaps as disturbing as the graphic depiction was his emphasis on mankind's love of primal violence. In both theme and development, Peckinpah was a sign of his times, anticipating the next generation of films and Americans' fascination with all things violent.

Many of *Blood Meridian*'s gunfights do recall the intensity and excruciating detail of slow-motion close-ups from *The Wild Bunch* (1969). Another similarity between McCarthy's novel and *The Wild Bunch* is the use of comically grotesque characters, portrayed so well by L. Q. Jones and Strother Martin as a pair of opportunistic scavengers seen going through the pockets of the dead. The most noticeable parallel between *Blood Meridian* and *The Wild Bunch* is that both depict a band of marauders roaming the countryside, loosely bound by self-serving interests. Peckinpah is more nostalgic than the McCarthy of *Blood Meridian* in giving characters formulaic roles, such as the old gunfighter as the last of a dying breed and the pastoral innocence of good country folk, the Mexican *campesinos*. At times, Peckinpah's sensibility is conventional and mythic, and thus closer to that of McCarthy's more recent westerns, the Border Trilogy. Most of Peckinpah's westerns—*Ride the High Country, Major Dundee,* and *Bring Me the Head of Alfredo Garcia*—demonstrate a pastoral love for small villages and rural life. The films offer us protagonists who live according to manly codes and who choose to die heroic, existential deaths. Despite their atavistic capacity for violence, Peckinpah characters also demonstrate a strong romantic streak and, in the end, heroically sacrifice themselves in a blaze of glory.

Glanton's gang has no such loyalties. When Black Jackson kills White Jackson by the campfire, the men move aside dumbly and continue eating, as if the matter has been settled according to their own laws of Darwinian justice. After the Yuma massacre, Tobin encourages the kid to shoot the judge while he has a chance. Near the beginning of *The Wild Bunch,* the gang's leader, played by William Holden, shoots a wounded man who, it is decided, must be left behind. Likewise, in *Blood Meridian* wounded members of the gang are left behind as part of the practical necessity of riding on. On several occasions Judge Holden explains the need for contests to the death. Thus, the kid's acts of mercy, or, as the judge calls them, "clemency," are considered as misplaced loyalty, a less natural sign of weakness, an unwillingness to participate in the violence of the gang. Even the ex-priest Tobin, whom one would expect to be merciful, lectures the kid about helping another gang member pull out an arrow because the wounded man might have retaliated like an animal: "Don't you know he'd of took you with him? . . . Like a bride to the altar" (163). At the novel's end, at Fort Griffin, the kid's survival instincts do fail when he does not sense any danger from Judge Holden.

Antimythic films from the Vietnam era depicting "the old ultraviolence" of war as satiric critiques of society include *Dr. Strangelove, Catch-22, Kelly's Heroes, M*A*S*H, Slaughterhouse Five,* and *Apocalypse Now.* The era's most popular revisionist western was Arthur Penn's *Little Big Man* (1970), which addressed many of the counterculture's social and historical critiques. Dustin Hoffman plays the main character, Jack Crabbe, a comic hero who systematically "deflates the standard Western roles of rescued captive, White Indian, scout, gunfighter, and gambler" (Slotkin, *Gunfighter* 631). Although the film is primarily a comic satire ridiculing western myths, the mood abruptly changes during the numbing violence of the Battle of the Washita, "when Custer and his men ride in over the white snowfields to massacre the village, mercilessly shooting Crabbe's wife and the infant on the cradle-board as she flees" (Slotkin, *Gunfighter* 631). For a Vietnam-era audience, especially after My Lai, the scene all too clearly parallels the brutality of American troops in Southeast Asia.

In a scene reminiscent of Richard Mulligan's portrayal of the jingoistic General Custer in *Little Big Man, Blood Meridian*'s pompous Captain White—an appropriate name for this character—rambles on about the supremacy of the white race while the kid politely listens without much comprehension. He is young and inexperienced and knows nothing about the recent war with Mexico. In contrast to Captain White and Judge Holden, the kid kills by instinct, savagely, in the heat of the moment, without forethought or rationale. As the kid sits by, dumbly waiting, the captain describes his elaborate plans for a grand filibustering expedition, rhapsodizing about Manifest Destiny and the duty of white men to wrest Sonora back from the Mexicans:

> What we are dealing with, he said, is a race of degenerates. A mongrel race little better than niggers. And maybe no better. There is no government in Mexico. Hell, there's no God in Mexico.[3] Never will be. We are dealing with a people manifestly incapable of governing themselves. And do you know what happens with people who cannot govern themselves? That's right. Others come in to govern for them. (34)

By conquering Sonora, Captain White concludes, "Americans will be able to get to California without having to pass through our benighted sister republic" (34). Like Custer in *Little Big Man,* the captain prides himself on making judgments that prove to be rash about the quality of men who will help him divide the spoils. As a reward for listening to this long-winded rhetoric, the captain announces that he finds potential in the kid: "You're young. But I don't misread you. I'm seldom mistaken in a man. I think you mean to make your mark in this world. Am I wrong?" (34–35). Meanwhile the blustery captain puts the recruiter asleep, and the kid remains little more than stunned by the confusing largess of the captain's strange theories. All he can manage to do is nervously rub "the palms of his hands on the knees of his filthy jeans" (35). There is more than a little of Dustin Hoffman's Jack Crabbe in the numb mindlessness of *Blood Meridian*'s kid. This scene also doubles later scenes between the kid and the judge in which the kid is also unable to comprehend the latter's elaborate philosophy of violence. Ironically, Captain White's racist screed at this point juxtaposes comically with his sudden defeat by the Comanches and his fate in Chihuahua as a severed head, bearing a mute, startled expression, preserved in a jar of mescal. The Comanche massacre, which McCarthy broadly labels "death hilarious," mocks Captain White's self-aggrandizing plans. Because of arrogance, Captain White—like Custer at the Little Big Horn—misjudges the tactical situation. Minutes before the massacre, he still believes his troop has chanced upon a dozen or so stock thieves, who will provide a "little sport" (51). The butchery that engulfs Captain White and his militia belittles White's rhetoric and exposes the fallacy of his rant about white supremacy.

The unpopular war in Vietnam caused many people to reassess American myths. Revisionists noted disturbing connections between American conquest along the frontier and the war in Vietnam. Free-fire zones, carpet bombing, and search-and-destroy missions were woefully similar to historical massacres at White Sands and Wounded Knee. On the killing fields of Vietnam, frontier nomenclature was commonly used by troops as battle slang: "Every grunt knew at least one bunch of refugee huts just outside the wire called 'Dogpatch,' one firebase called 'the Alamo,' one provincial town called 'Dodge City,' one part of the boundary that marked the way to 'Indian country'" (Beidler 8). Such terms indicated soldiers' ironic identification of themselves as mythic cowboys and the Vietnamese as Indians, albeit in a very different frontier. The late sixties forced many Americans, especially students and teachers, to reject old myths and frankly reassess the brutal facts of nationalism. The climbing death toll and the planeloads of body bags bore awful "witness to the end of America's absolute confidence in its moral exclusivity, its military invincibility, its manifest destiny.... With the young men who died in Vietnam died the dream of an American century" (Karnow 9). James Oliver Robertson, in a wide-ranging study of American culture, argues that the violence of Vietnam rapidly altered the mythos of many younger Americans and intellectuals:

> The horror and the holocaust, the actual hell of war, which Americans had come to disregard . . . were literally brought home to many. . . .
>
> In the face of the actualities of the war being fought—visible through television, reported in the newspapers, or told by returning soldiers—the idea that the Vietnam War was part of an important total global war became difficult to maintain. Americans began to see the story as illogical, unreal: a myth. (340)

Like other intellectuals, historians played an important part in this ideological realignment. Richard Hofstadter and Michael Wallace, coeditors of *American Violence* (1970), described the era as "a time of unprecedented concern over American violence" (v). Hofstadter predicted, "The rediscovery of our violence will undoubtedly be one of the important intellectual legacies of the 1960s" (3). Until the Vietnam atrocities and civil unrest, America had a sort of "historical amnesia" that made it "hard to conceive of violence as a subject at all" (3–4). The change in perspective was so dramatic that Hofstadter and Wallace anticipated the revisionist histories that would follow the Vietnam era:

> In the future, no doubt, much of this inattention [to violence] will be remedied. Today we are not only aware of our own violence; we are frightened by it. We are now quite ready to see that there is far more violence in our national heritage than our proud, sometimes smug, national self-image admits of. Our violence frightens us, as it frightens others, because in our singular position uncontrolled domestic violence coincides with unparalleled national power. (5)

Hofstadter and Wallace's thesis directs attention to a reassessment of the "extraordinary frequency" of American violence—"its sheer commonplaceness in our history, its persistence into the very recent and contemporary times, and its rather abrupt contrast with our pretensions to singular national virtue" (7). They find that the frontier myth of consensus ideology contributed to the "historical amnesia" since it focused on heroes and progress, while racial, religious, and class violence in the cities was largely ignored. Some historians reacted to Vietnam with a kind of "inverted Turnerism," like Joe B. Frantz in "The Frontier Tradition: An Invitation to Violence," which both "condemns western violence as the root of our present troubles and apologizes for that violence as a necessary instrument of American progress" (qtd. in Slotkin, *Gunfighter Nation* 558). Describing American exceptionalism, Louis Hartz called the historical record "vivid with bloodshed" and "violent energy" that spread throughout American society from the frontier (qtd. in Slotkin, *Gunfighter Nation* 557). As Hofstadter and Wallace predicted, many historians of the last three decades have indeed distanced themselves from the Turner thesis and its reliance on Jefferson's agrarian dream of progress. Turner's thesis of the frontier as a vacant land dominated by American exceptionalism has been replaced in post-Vietnam years with a "widowed land" perspective more critical of the racial violence so evident during all phases of European conquest.

W. Eugene Hollon, in *Frontier Violence* (1974), echoes this emerging view when he states, "America has always had a violent past, and the frontier in a way has stood for this country at its most violent" (vii). Hollon's list of brutal western figures includes almost everyone:

> a wide range of individual types—claim jumpers, miners, cowboys, cattle rustlers, Indian haters, Border ruffians, Mexican banditti, mule skinners, railroad workers, highwaymen, racial bigots of various colors, professional outlaws, homicidal maniacs, and hired gunslingers. Each group had more than a speaking acquaintance with violence, for the rough life on the frontier prior to 1900 produced scant recognition of the law as law.
>
> In addition, there were so-called "gentlemen of property and standing"—ranchers, farmers, bankers, town builders, railroad owners, lawyers, doctors, politicians, mine operators and others—who sometimes took the law into their own hands. They generally operated in the West as self-appointed members of mobs. (vii)

In an observation that could apply equally well to the world of *Blood Meridian*, Hollon writes that "evidence of violence on the Western frontier is so overwhelming that the innumerable examples overshadow the deeper causes" (viii). Hollon's study, as would be expected in a history of the immediate post-Vietnam and Civil Rights era, looks at violence "particularly as it related to Indians, Mexicans, Negroes, and Chinese" (ix). Hollon is one of the first to apply the term "genocide" to frontier history in a chapter entitled "Genocide—or Manifest Destiny?" and his scathing conclusion is that "from the Pequot War in Colonial New England to the massacre at Wounded Knee in South Dakota on December 29, 1890, the twin strains—civilization and extermination—marched side by side through American history" (129).[4]

During this era many intellectuals embraced the sociobiological concept of man as hunter. Building on the work of Raymond Dart, other sociobiologists linked modern human behavior with a bloodthirsty past. In the mid-seventies E. O. Wilson and Desmond Morris began to claim "a number of traits as genetically based and therefore human universals, including territoriality" as a "product of our evolutionary hunting past" (Sussman 4). Echoing the sociobiologists, Joseph Campbell, in *Myths to Live By* (1972), pointed to the evidence of warlike tribes' ability to survive by outcompeting more peaceful cultures. Myths of violence, of man as hunter and warrior, are simply part of the Darwinian "universal struggle for existence" (169–70).

One probable major source for the theme, tone, and imagery of *Blood Meridian* is T. R. Fehrenbach's historical study, *Comanches: The Destruction of a People* (1974). Like others during the Vietnam era, Fehrenbach reassesses the extreme violence of mankind's beginnings and its continuing effect as a historical force:

> History is brutal; only future peril lies in omitting or obscuring man's continuing brutalities. Generations that have been sheltered from the brutalities of the past are poorly equipped to cope with those of their own times. The story of the People is a brutal story, and its judgments must be brutal. These judgments may offend those who would have man be a different kind of being, and the world a different sort of place. (xv)

Much of the language of this book is paralleled in *Blood Meridian*; I suspect McCarthy's copy of *Comanches* is well worn, with many passages highlighted. As John Sepich has demonstrated, McCarthy has meticulously researched the historical details in the novel. Fehrenbach's ideas and language describing early man and primitive origins are suggestive of Judge Holden's speeches on the primal nature of man, such as the observation that "cultures always reveal their essential natures in warfare" (253). Throughout the study, Fehrenbach lectures his readers about the hard lessons of war as depicted in the brutal history of North American tribes. He describes how Indians moving into the Americas "appropriated what was then a manless, primordial wilderness" in an "endless pursuit and slaughter of other living creatures"; "they were man the hunter, man the killer, then and now the most dangerous and formidable creature ever to appear on a four-billion-year-old earth" (4–5). Fehrenbach paints a violent Darwinian vision of the world:

> Grubbing, hunting, killing, feasting, mating, dying and giving birth, exulting in the new moon of spring, browning under the harsh wind and brazen summer sun, moaning beneath the hungry winter snows, they were different from modern man only in circumstance. . . . They knew hope, fear, ecstasy, love, disillusion, and despair, and occasionally they found time for wonder. They were not free creatures: they were hounded by a hundred dark dreads and fearful taboos. They sensed mystery in their existence and in the universe and they tried desperately to find some meaning in it all; they strove to see and understand the cosmic forces that ruled the physical world so that they might bend them to their needs and wishes, the basis of all human religion. . . . Seeing the sun rise, the moon set, the red fire throw giant black shadows on their cavern walls, at bay or in exaltation, these men and women felt the same things felt by modern man. (5–6)

Note the use of phrases such as "mystery in their existence," and the poetic description of the sun and moon and fire and shadows, all images that are prevalent throughout *Blood Meridian*. As one carefully considers Fehrenbach's stark, dystopian worldview, his prehistoric bands of aborigines begin to sound very similar to Glanton's gang in their nomadic wanderings: "The land was hard on man and beast; it made all life upon it volatile and restless, cruel but hardy, ever-moving. . . . They had little opportunity to pause or wonder, to chart the heavens or to think about the sum of things. . . . Home was where they camped" (22). Even Fehrenbach's violent poetry of western landscape resembles the language of *Blood Meridian*:

> [The winds] blew free, now south, now north, in constant warfare that set off great electrical displays and generated black funnel clouds, tornadoes that sometimes dipped and tore the earth. . . . It was a country of terrible meteorological change, blazing in deep summer under a brazen sun that made the distant bluff sides dance in shimmering heat, shivering in winter under ice storms that howled off the roof of the world and froze the earth under scudding clouds and the low-slung moon. (21–22)

Fehrenbach refers to the "blinding sky and distant, vague horizons" and compares the plains to the sea (296). His chapter titles echo phrases from *Blood Meridian*: "Death in the High Country," "Smoke and Tears," "Blood on the Moon," and "The Graveyard Plains." These chapters document numerous examples of mutilation by scalping, raping, tearing off genitals, and other "bloody melee" (285). Perhaps even McCarthy's inspiration for a title came from Fehrenbach, as the word "meridian" is used in discussing the "ninety-eighth meridian" within a chapter entitled "Blood on the Moon" (296). By itself this might be a coincidence, but other words parallel McCarthy's text also: *blood, bloody, bloodthirst, bloodlust, mystery, mysteries, mysterious,* and *meridian* appear throughout Fehrenbach's text.

The most significant parallel between *Blood Meridian* and *Comanches* is the similarity of the massacre of Captain White's militia to Fehrenbach's three historical descriptions of Comanche warfare. Fehrenbach describes in detail a battle in the summer of 1758, when a Spanish mission, San Saba, was attacked by Comanche warriors. Like the soldiers of *Blood Meridian,* one of the padres is so astonished he cannot speak:

> Padre Molina . . . was made speechless by what he saw. Two thousand Indians, all mounted warriors, were slowly riding around the walls. Although the Spaniards did not recognize them, these warriors were Comanches and Wichitas. . . . The savages were a breathtaking, barbaric spectacle—Plains Amerindians in the full panoply of war. The long lines of riders wore fantastic headdresses of plumes, deer antlers, and bison horns. (202)

When a nearby Spanish fort sent a contingent of soldiers to defend the mission, "there was a brief, bloody melee. The Spaniards were shot or lanced to a man. Only one, badly wounded, was able to crawl to cover" (203). This scene, when joined with a description of a "complete rout" of Spanish forces later that year, closely matches McCarthy's Comanche massacre. T. J. Owen's description of the battle of Plum Creek in 1840 fills in more details:

> It was a spectacle never to be forgotten, the wild, fantastic band as they stood in battle array. . . . Both horses and riders were decorated most profusely, with all the beauty and horror of their wild taste

combined. Red ribbons streamed out from their horses' tails as
they swept around us, riding fast.... There was a huge warrior,
who wore a stovepipe hat, and another who wore a fine pigeon-
tailed cloth coat, buttoned up behind. Some wore on their heads
immense buck and buffalo horns . . . (qtd. in Fehrenbach 334)

Fehrenbach includes an engraving of the battle by T. J. Owen depicting the unnerving incongruities of Comanche dress: a warrior wears a stovepipe hat and holds an umbrella (344). This image doubles with McCarthy's description of Comanche warriors, "one in a stovepipe hat and one with an umbrella" (*Blood Meridian* 52). As one reads Fehrenbach's study, the parallels between his description of the Comanches and McCarthy's are obvious and striking. The timing of the book's publication in 1974 coincides with McCarthy's move to El Paso (Woodward 31). In addition, Fehrenbach's book was published by Knopf, which has also been McCarthy's publisher. Given that McCarthy is a regional writer who relies on exacting historical detail, and given the lapse of years between his novels, it is reasonable to posit that McCarthy spent considerable time researching Indians and frontier conditions. Noting all the similarities between Fehrenbach's study and McCarthy's poetic application is not meant, of course, to detract from the greatness of *Blood Meridian*—as the author himself has commented, tongue in cheek, "The ugly fact is books are made out of books" (Woodward 31).

We can evaluate McCarthy's possible debt to revisionist history of the West, which anticipated the movement now labeled the New Western History, by considering a major figure in that school, Patricia Nelson Limerick.[5] As she writes in *The Legacy of Conquest* (1987), "Reorganized, the history of the West is a study of a place undergoing conquest and never fully escaping its consequences. . . . Conquest forms the historical bedrock of the whole nation" (26–27). It is a "process very similar to what happened all around the planet where Europeans appeared and struggled with the natives, and when the dust settled, the natives had much less" (Limerick, "Borderland" 8). Limerick believes that this past, and our view of it, definitely affects the present:

In incident after incident, whites on punitive expeditions set out
to kill Indians—possibly the Indians who had committed the theft

> or attack about to be avenged, and possibly not. In times of tension, individuals appeared as categories—hostile until proven friendly and, even if friendly, still alien.
>
> One would be happy to consign this pattern of thought to the old frontier West, but the quarantine would not hold. (*Legacy of Conquest* 349)

McCarthy's extreme violence is most likely beyond the pale of what Limerick has in mind. Despite *Blood Meridian*'s representation of "ideas of savagery and civilization" (*Legacy of Conquest* 25), the novel is not, as some critics have suggested, on a revisionist tack, at least not as revisionism is defined by New Western Historians. *Blood Meridian* does debunk the mythos of what Limerick calls the "presumption of innocence and exceptionalism [that] is interwoven with the roots of frontier history" ("Adventures" 74). Limerick finds that the old progress myth "blurs the fact of conquest and throws a veil over the similarities between the story of American westward expansion and the planetary story of the expansion of European empires" (75). The popular myth "carries a persistently happy affect, a tone of adventure, heroism, and even fun very much in contrast with the tough, complicated, and sometimes bloody and brutal realities of conquest" (75). *Blood Meridian*'s historical vision of Limerick's "bloody and brutal realities" is expanded exponentially. New Western revisionists' focus on Anglo-American conquest is not akin to McCarthy's all-encompassing vision of man's pervasive genetic propensities for violence. In McCarthy's worldview, savagery is independent of race; massacres in *Blood Meridian* are committed by Indians as well as whites. Whereas New Western Historians weigh Anglo-American conquest on the scales of civilized sensibilities—with a strong cultural impetus of American brutalities in Vietnam—McCarthy, like many anthropologists and biologists, weighs it against the evolutionary history of violence. In the long speeches of Judge Holden, whose blatant atrocities shock even the other gang members, violence is rationalized as man's natural birthright. The judge's mad exuberance, his dancing and fiddling, celebrates a warrior's ancient blood rite. Whereas New Western Historians condemn atrocities predicated on racial superiority, McCarthy's novel presents an even more uncomfortable paradigm: an investigation of man's innate capacity for genocide. The literary accomplishment of *Blood Meridian* is as spellbinding as his frontier history is repellent. What disturbs us most, perhaps, is that there is finally no heroic protagonist, no narrative Gulliver to condemn the "whole damned human race" to oblivion.

Forrest G. Robinson summarizes the pre-Vietnam tendency in American culture as the "inability to look for long at the most painful chapters of the western American story" (92). Given the post-Vietnam perspective of New Western History, Henry Nash Smith, best known for his consensus study *Virgin Land,* later admitted failing "to give proper attention to Indians" and "'the grimly ironic later history' of Manifest Destiny," which he referred to as the "national 'cult of violence'" with "legacies of racism and environmental abuse" (Robinson 89). The awful realism of *Blood Meridian* is echoed in Robinson's view of western history in general: "What Smith describes as 'the tragic dimensions of the Westward Movement' are at once unbearable and unforgettable; we try to press them from sight and mind, but they are always there, on the margins, ready to spring back to view" (92).

McCarthy springs the "unbearable and unforgettable" on us as no other western writer before. Nothing in the conventional myths of Anglo progress prepares us for the myth-shattering effects of *Blood Meridian.* Since the Vietnam era, the popular desire to entertain ourselves with excessive, aleatory violence has continued to escalate. In the mass media, the beginning of sensational fictionalized violence may be traced to the cult films known as "roughies." Such mid-sixties films as *Blood Feast, White Slaves of Chinatown, Olga's House of Shame, Love Camp 7,* and *Mantis in Lace* played off the 1960 hit *Psycho* by showing naked women tortured and knifed by sadistic villains (J. R. Peterson 172). As a result of the immense success of these marginal horror flicks, slasher films such as *The Texas Chainsaw Massacre* became standard fare as second features at late-night drive-ins.

The first of the new breed of serious Hollywood films to borrow their methods, and the first to directly challenge the Production Code, was Arthur Penn's *Bonnie and Clyde* (1967), starring Warren Beatty and Fay Dunaway. It graphically depicted wounds never seen before on film by using realistic blood—and lots of it. In 1966 the Code was revised so that such films would include the warning "Suggested for Mature Audiences" (Miller 204). Although the revised code still issued mandates to filmmakers, controversial new work began to break down the code's restrictions. Along with *Bonnie and Clyde, Blow-Up* (1966), *Bedazzled* (1967), *Barbarella* (1968) and the Sergio Leone westerns starring Clint Eastwood all pushed the boundaries of "decency" (Miller 208). Although the war in Vietnam and the live footage of mass media coverage had prepared the public for more realistic violence in films, critics were still shocked in 1967 at the open vulgarities of *The Dirty Dozen,* which "ignited a fierce controversy over violence on screen" and was blamed for inciting the Detroit race riots (Miller 209). The *New York Times* predicted that such violence would "deaden [the public's] sensitivities and make slaughter seem a meaningless cliché" (Miller 209). Hollywood was under pressure from both sides of the controversy. Filmmakers wanted more artistic freedom and insisted they were producing popular films more in keeping with changing times; conservative forces, including parents and politicians, were pushing for more controls and warnings. In 1968, Jack Valenti, president of the Motion Picture Association, officially ended the Production Code and replaced it with the new ratings system. Shortly after its release, Hollywood instituted the present rating system, which included an X for violence. With the new system, a rash of R-rated films, and a few X-rated ones, such as *Midnight Cowboy* (1969) and *A Clockwork Orange* (1970), were produced in a milieu where a growing number of people not only accepted the new aesthetics but grew hungry for it (Miller 210).

In the years since Vietnam, America has also fought an undeclared war in the streets, losing more of its citizens to crime in the last twenty years than in all foreign wars: half a million murdered and 2.5 million injured (Schlosser 38). For American culture in the second half of the twentieth century, the war in Vietnam did become a watershed event, prompting an intellectual revision but also a degradation of social conditions. The escalation of violence in Vietnam and the corresponding violence at home were clarion calls for new ways of thinking. Old myths and plotlines would no longer work. Film directors began to reassess the character of American violence. Doctors and professors began to look for its biological, psychological, chemical, and historical roots; new studies were begun on rape, murder, battering, genocide, and war. It was as if the nation was demanding to know who or what agent should be held responsible, who should carry the stigma of blame.

Two experiments in psychology conducted in the early seventies seemed to clinch the matter. Philip Zimbardo's prison study in 1973 demonstrated how quickly young men assumed violent personas. Ordinary college students volunteered to be part of a "guards and prisoners" scenario, with roles assigned randomly. One third of the guards soon developed abusive patterns of behavior. Zimbardo's study demonstrated how quickly an individual's personality could be replaced by a group identity—even if that new identity demanded extreme aggression (Zimbardo 38–40). These findings reinforced Stanley Milgram's famous "electric shock" experiment in 1963 on the power of authority versus personal ethics. Participants in the study were randomly assigned the roles of teachers or learners. As a learner unavoidably made errors on a simple vocabulary test, the teacher was instructed to apply increasingly severe electric shocks as lessons. Although the electric shock machines were in reality inoperable, the learners played their roles convincingly by writhing in pain, screaming, and pleading to be released as the shocks became more intense. Teachers applying the shocks fully believed that learners were experiencing real pain. A number of psychiatrists had predicted that only one in a thousand of the volunteers would continue applying shocks past dangerous levels all the way up to the maximum point on the gauge, ominously labeled XXX. In fact, about two-thirds of those tested continued applying shocks to the maximum level, impervious to screams or pleas for mercy. Milgram's point had been made: normal people respond by obeying the specific demands of assigned roles even if those roles require sadistic behavior. Milgram's experiment has been repeated around the world on thousands of volunteers, and the percentage of people willing to apply the maximum shock consistently remains between 60 and 90 percent. Even innovative pleas for mercy on the part of learners, such as complaining of heart attacks or collapsing in apparent death, have not changed the general results (Milgram, *Obedience to Authority*).

Ironically, one undeniable cultural response to the violence of Vietnam has been the escalating graphic depiction of atavistic violence in films and on TV. Also, much of popular entertainment—from video games to laser tag to paint guns—has slanted toward violence explicitly produced for the sake of vicarious sensation. For fifty cents, step right up and kill a hundred aliens, or a hundred humans for that matter! Instead of the once-vaunted dream of world peace, popular culture in the Information Age celebrates a cult of violence. The violence of the sixties was like a first exhilarating experience with drugs—fun but often leading to addiction, with each new horror film or video game, like another hit, increasing our tolerance, stimulating our need for more. Like post-traumatic stress disorder, paradoxically, our viewing of media violence grows in proportion to our exposure to real violence. Violence begets violence in a Girardian escalation in which reality and fiction soon become indistinguishable. It is a bad case of monkey see, monkey do.

All of these complex responses were already incipient by the late 1960s and early '70s. Norman Mailer's *Armies of the Night* and *Why Are We in Vietnam?,* Kurt Vonnegut's *Slaughterhouse Five* and *Breakfast of Champions,* and Joseph Heller's *Catch-22* sought broad social changes by underscoring the absurd state of American authority in government and the military-industrial complex. Politicians, generals, and corporate executives—along with anyone over thirty—seemed part of a vast conspiracy. Mailer noted that Vietnam was becoming its own worst parody, "more like *Naked Lunch*—an experience not so much apocalyptic in any absolute sense . . . just loud, violent, crazed, and lurid" (qtd. in Beidler 12). The laugh reflex was combined with horror into a new ultraviolent pastiche of the "dreadful, funny, nightmarish, ecstatic" (Beidler 12). Given such a national climate, the old reliable frontier myths of American progress, dressed in the conservative cloth of American exceptionalism, appeared absurdly inadequate. In an epigraph to *Born on the Fourth of July* (1976), Ron Kovic catches the bitter irony of the new revisionism when he returned home from Vietnam, demoralized and disillusioned after severe injuries:

> I am your yankee doodle dandy
> your john wayne come home
> your fourth of july firecracker
> exploding in your grave.
>   (qtd. in Beidler 161)

BLOOD MERIDIAN AND THE REASSESSMENT OF VIOLENCE

We could do worse than read the violence of *Blood Meridian*. Our stories reflect our culture, telling us in effect, "This is who you are—make the necessary changes." But we would rather not see ourselves as bloodthirsty predators. We love quick sensations, feeling good, feeling bad, feeling something and feeling it fast, that video-sports-advertising-CNN-MTV-postmodern world, where myth sells better than history. Despite the furor over Vietnam, and its cultural fallout, the progress myth is once again being bottled and sold to the youth market—to those too young to remember the horrific images of real violence but young enough to enjoy the show. Somehow, the rips and tears of the old conservative consensus have been mended, and the very generation that protested a bad war has grown up to sell new wars. It is not, to be sure, the 1950s reborn but rather a facsimile bearing the moniker "The American Century," indicating a new consensus about our own millennial preeminence in world affairs. American confidence has been reformatted and upgraded. Long live the full moon, the bright noontime pinnacle of American achievement and blue-chip Internet stocks. May we always be ascendant, on a bull run, and in our buying frenzy, once again forget the old ghosts of mindless violence, "red in tooth and claw," out there in the night, at our borders, in our streets, on the prowl.

Three

Blood Meridian and Literary Naturalism

> Human beings now find themselves in a material universe that defies their comprehension and control, knowledge and certainty giving way to indeterminacy and uncertainty.—Paul Civello

Blood Meridian can be viewed as part of the continuing American tradition of literary naturalism, a movement best remembered in American fiction in turn-of-the-century writers, including Ambrose Bierce, Stephen Crane, Theodore Dreiser, Hamlin Garland, Jack London, Frank Norris, and Upton Sinclair. Scholars such as Paul Civello and Donald Pizer, however, have demonstrated that literary naturalism can be traced through the modern period into postmodern literature. Civello's *American Literary Naturalism and Its Twentieth-Century Transformations* documents naturalistic elements through the work of Ernest Hemingway and Don DeLillo. Pizer's *Twentieth-Century American Literary Naturalism: An Interpretation* traces it through the work of John Steinbeck, Saul Bellow, and Norman Mailer. Pizer believes literary naturalism appears in stories during times of cultural stress as "a sure sign that writers have again sensed that 'hard times' are here" (*Theory and Practice* 186). Writers who envision hard times in naturalistic terms share several characteristics:

1. A Darwinian worldview, emphasizing ruthless competition and survival of the fittest in harsh environments as well as random accidents in an uncaring universe.

2. Realism in speech and action, using regional dialects and historical details.
3. Amoral, arrogant characters involved in ironic, absurd circumstances.
4. Comic, grotesque images of wounded or misshapen humanity.
5. A prevailing mood of pessimistic determinism in nineteenth-century naturalism and a sense of pessimistic uncertainty in contemporary naturalism.

An early study of the movement by Lars Ahnebrink, *The Beginnings of Naturalism in American Fiction,* describes how late in the nineteenth century many American writers began to tire of romanticism's roseate dream. Hamlin Garland found it full of stifling clichés and worn images: "The West had become the Golden West, the land of wealth and freedom and happiness. Vast sweeps of untracked prairies, whose grasses waved like a sea; lakes in whose depths cool groves were mirrored; droves of elk and deer and antelope; rushing rivers on whose banks stood vine-decked cottages—these were the sunny vistas of the songs" (qtd. in Ahnebrink 12). By the 1890s, realism came to be prized as a more authentic style by a generation of gritty, muckraking journalists who were forging a new kind of story with American landscapes and naturalistic themes. Of this group, Ambrose Bierce was the first to break with his era's Victorian conventions. His experiences in the Civil War changed his outlook on life, leading him to write dark satires about the grotesque images of war. He adopted a cynical, hard-edged persona, for which he is remembered as "Bitter Bierce." Bierce's ironic poses and surrealism anticipate the next generation of naturalists and early moderns.

Although naturalism took root in America in the 1890s and reached its popular zenith in the work of Stephen Crane and Jack London, for over two decades it had been fashionable in France, where Darwin's ideas were readily accepted by intellectuals. Emile Zola's novels became the primary model for American naturalists, as both Stephen Crane and Frank Norris read him early in their careers and subsequently took on many of his ideas, transplanting Zola's structures to American settings. Ahnebrink notes, "The basic philosophy of literary naturalism was deterministic and positivistic and consequently the naturalists focused their interests on the external reality. Darwin's interpretation of the mechanism of the universe, the positivism of Comte, and Marx's socialism were adopted by the naturalistic school" (22). The urgent need to inject social realism into fiction gave American authors artistic permission to write about taboo subjects involving the lower classes. Often, there is an implicit exposé as these writers depict wrenching scenes of poverty and depredation. For the poor, survival in a brutal environment is shown to be a struggle for daily bread, with Darwinian forces pushing debased characters to desperate acts. The social conditions of the frontier and urban slums are depicted as wild jungles in which primal instincts dominate. Fear, greed, and lust rule mankind. In hostile environments, humans act from mammalian instinct, playing out an endless and deadly cycle of predator and prey. Pizer describes the subject of naturalism as "the closed and destructive mechanistic and Darwinian world of struggle" (*Cambridge Companion* 10). George J. Becker notes naturalism's "pessimistic materialistic determinism" in which the forces of "heredity and environment" determine "behavior and belief" (qtd. in Pizer, *Realism and Naturalism* 12). Pizer emphasizes the movement's "violence and passion . . . which culminate in desperate moments and violent death" and lead to "the extraordinary and excessive in human nature" (*Realism and Naturalism* 13).

Denis Donoghue's description of McCarthy's characters as "recently arrived primates, each possessing a spinal column but little or no capacity of mind or consciousness" (5) captures the apish nature of *Blood Meridian*'s characters, as does Ahnebrink's portrait of naturalism's stereotypical characters: "indolent and dull, devoid of free will and purpose, sensual, and often abnormal . . . creatures dominated by their instincts" (28). The predominance of the ape metaphor in naturalism probably has roots in Charles Darwin's suggestion of the connection in *The Descent of Man* (1874). As John Sepich (146) demonstrates, McCarthy uses the "ape" metaphor as a recurring motif throughout *Blood Meridian*: Mexican bandits "pummel one another like apes" (65); prisoners "picked at themselves like apes" (74); the gang at one point lives on raw meat "without fire or bread or camaraderie any more than banded apes" (148); and after the Yuma massacre, the survivors gather at a water hole to drink "like rival bands of apes" (284). The old ape nature of mankind is never far from the surface. The gang members appear as "Neolithic herdsmen," often shambling, grunting, and spitting (288). As they "ride on" through the high wilderness, they increasingly take on animal aspects, "slouched under slickers hacked from greasy halfcured hides and so cowled in these primitive skins before the gray and driving rain they looked like wardens of some dim sect sent forth to proselytize among the very beasts of the land" (187). And in the night the "wolves in the dark forests of the world below called to them as if they were friends to man" (188). When we see Judge Holden dancing naked, sweating by a fire, or scalping a boy who ten minutes before sat complacently on his knee, his bestiality seems strangely juxtaposed with what we know of his interest in science and his loquacious familiarity with several languages. But Holden's civility and acquaintance with cities masks a primal nature; there is no softening or obscuring of Darwinian law. He suggests that the best education for children would be to put them "in a pit with wild dogs" in order "to puzzle out . . . one of three doors that does not harbor wild lions. They should be made to run naked in the desert" (146). When ex-priest Tobin, representing the church and civilized ethics, protests such savagery, the judge responds with a defense from nature's theology: "If God meant to interfere in the degeneracy of mankind would he not have done so by now? Wolves cull themselves, man. What other creature could? And is the race of man not more predacious yet?" (146). The judge, who takes on the role of ideological narrator, answers his own rhetorical questions by reiterating the theme of "mindless violence" in a statement that alludes to the title:

> The way of the world is to bloom and to flower and die but in the affairs of men there is no waning and the noon of his expression signals the onset of night. His spirit is exhausted at the peak of his achievement. His meridian is at once his darkening and the evening of his day. (146–47)

Man has surpassed wolves and all other predators on his climb up the food chain, and as a consequence of successful competition, has reached an obsessive, crazed pinnacle of savagery. He is a clever genetic strain—a predator species run amok, crazy like a young elephant in rut who kills in bloodlust. The nineteenth-century naturalistic theme of *Blood Meridian* converges with twentieth-century theories on the origins of mankind's violence. Social biologists Barbara Ehrenreich (*Blood Rites*) and Richard Wrangham and Dale Peterson (*Demonic Males*) offer compelling arguments for *Homo sapiens*' genetic propensity for what can accurately be described as essentially ape traits, with humans, chimpanzees, and gorillas included in the same family grouping, known as Hominidae (if we accept the reclassification proposed by Ian Tattersall and others). All three species share the capacity for extreme violence, including murder. We all bear the mark of Cain. Even at the culmination of evolutionary achievement, mankind is still apish, willing to kill—for anger, greed, love, pride. And more than ever, mankind is capable of indiscriminate mass killing. All of McCarthy's work up through *Blood Meridian* depicts mankind's apish nature as ugly and rapacious, juxtaposed against conventional romantic or religious notions of earth's "perfect china sky" (147). Cathedrals and priests are destroyed, the earth bears testament to geologic violence, and characters like the kid and Judge Holden cannot be civilized out of violence; it is part of their dark nature, an ever-looming fate, a bloody meridian which precludes any kind of idealistic saving grace. According to the judge, man's feeble attempts at morality, like the kid's "clemency," are historically only signs of weakness that allow atavistic men an advantage in the game of survival.

When one of the gang members declares, like philosopher Jean-Jacques Rousseau, that "might does not make right" and that "combat is not vindicated morally," the judge only smiles and replies with a brutal truth: "Moral law is an invention of mankind for the disenfranchisement of the powerful in favor of the weak. Historical law subverts it at every turn" (250). The judge goes on to argue that survival is always the genetic baseline, as it is nature's only "ultimate test," whereas particular moral arguments, no matter how logical or civilized, can never be proven right or wrong. According to naturalism's deterministic philosophy, the "chambers of the historically absolute" have always decided on the grounds of survival, making ethics trivial and of "little moment" as "moral right rendered void and without warrant." The judge speaks the literal truth of evolutionary naturalism, which, in its lowest common denominator, is "life and death, . . . what shall be and what shall not" (250). The individual dramas of each struggle for life double as the larger struggle of whole species: "There is room on the stage for one beast and one alone. All others are destined for a night that is eternal and without name. One by one they will step down into the darkness before the footlamps. Bears that dance, bears that don't" (331). And mankind, as the earth's most successful predator, continues to outcompete and outkill other species to extinction in a monomaniacal swath, destroying whole ecologies and altering the global environment. The judge pointedly notes that even the ex-priest Tobin can see the truth of such an argument since he has turned from the church and taken up killing. The ultimate extension of this crazed Babel of killing, of course, is that we might finally engage in mindless violence to the point of extinguishing ourselves. Man the killer becomes man the extinct. And this line of thought, this inevitable natural result of man's existence, is the naturalistic theme that McCarthy thrusts at us. We are forced to witness the thematic motif of primal violence as the body count goes up on every page. And in the second half of the novel, the judge patiently explains the philosophy behind what we are witnessing. As the judge's rhetoric increasingly intrudes upon the primary narrative, he takes on the metafictional quality of an author-figure.

Ahnebrink notes that the world inhabited by naturalistic characters is full of "vice, malice, wickedness" and that the "outcome of life" is "hopeless sorrow, sometimes stolid resignation; often with no other end than annihilation" (28). Stephen Crane's best-known novel, *The Red Badge of Courage,* exploded onto the American scene with more attention and controversy than *Blood Meridian* (which sold only about fifteen hundred copies in its first printing); some critics demanded its retraction, outraged by its graphic portrayals of violence and unpatriotic sentiments (Ahnebrink 98). Many naturalistic novels have likewise met with puzzled and angry reactions. In a review of Frank Norris's *McTeague,* we hear the same shock and horror that contemporary readers express over *Blood Meridian*: "It is a misfortune that he should have devoted so much skill and virility to the description of a life so essentially without spiritual significance and so repulsive in habit and quality. . . . The reader is immersed in a world of bald and brutal realism from beginning to end, and is brought into association with none whose vulgarity and brutality is relieved by higher qualities" (qtd. in Ahnebrink 115–16). Upton Sinclair's *The Jungle* provoked a national furor over the corruption and scandals within the meatpacking industry, which wasn't what Sinclair considered the novel's main theme. His naturalistic portrait of an immigrant family chewed and swallowed by the cruel machinery of capitalism went unnoticed by his turn-of-the-century audience. Given the tempering agency of time, it is possible that in a hundred years McCarthy's *Blood Meridian* might appear as a twentieth-century classic, no more shocking than *The Red Badge of Courage* or *McTeague* are to us today.

Wade Hall refers to *Blood Meridian* as "a grotesque theatre of the absurd" without elaborating on the novel as part of the long tradition of the American grotesque ("Human Comedy" 50), which Ahnebrink identifies as the primary image of literary naturalism. To exemplify the concept, consider this description from *The Red Badge of Courage* of a sergeant shot through the cheeks: "Its supports being injured, his jaw hung afar down, disclosing in the wide cavern of his mouth a pulsing mass of blood and teeth. And with it all he made attempts to cry out" (Crane, *Red Badge* 364). In the grotesque tradition characters are exaggerated into extreme shapes that parody human forms. Midgets and giants and various physical deformities warp classical human beauty into forms of comic absurdity. They serve as reminders that we all are, to one degree or another, in our faults comic grotesques. For instance, Norris's character McTeague is a giant with an immense square-cut head and huge hands whose ill-formed verbal retort is always, "You can't make small of me."

Sherwood Anderson's vision of the grotesque image in small midwestern towns is portrayed in *Winesburg, Ohio*. According to the pastoral agrarian myth, most succinctly defined in early American literature by Thomas Jefferson a hundred years before Anderson, small farming communities were believed to be retainers of the much-prized republican "virtue," which included domestic comforts, manly pursuits, and civilized restraint. Jefferson idealized the West as a land where opportunity would be unlimited for at least a thousand years, to be slowly populated with rugged farmers whose stable communities would be founded upon the premise of working close to the land while maintaining strong families. Anderson's collection of stories, however, shatters the agrarian myth of the American heartland by displaying a typical midwestern town full of grotesques, mocking Keatsian romantic notions of truth as beauty: "Man made the truths himself and each truth was a composite of a great many vague thoughts. It was the truths that made the people grotesques. . . . the moment one of the people took one of the truths to himself, called it his truth, and tried to live his life by it, he became a grotesque and the truth he embraced became a falsehood" (Anderson 23–24). In fact, Anderson's theory of the grotesque calls into question, like much of literary criticism today, the very phenomena of human imagination and language. All systems of belief, no matter how true, ultimately become absurdly exaggerated comic grotesques, which, paradoxically, attract as well as repel us with their unsightly proportions. The bizarre image of a grotesque—such as Captain White's head in a jar of mescal—compels us to look more closely, to see ourselves distorted in the jar, yet we want to avert our eyes, following our mother's advice, "Don't stare." In describing Crane's and London's novels, Paula Uruburu notices the same duality we find in McCarthy's work: we are "attracted, fascinated, without knowing why and yet repelled, wishing perhaps unconsciously to confront the monsters of the mind made flesh, while at the same time, wanting to run away from them" (84).

Ambrose Bierce's stories also develop the American grotesque with characters driven by base impulses that result in comic absurdity. His stories demonstrate how mankind's arrogance leads to the absurd surreality of war. In "Chickamauga" a small deaf child watches uncomprehendingly as wounded soldiers crawl away from the battle: "All their faces were singularly white and many were streaked and gouted with red. Something in this—something too perhaps, in their grotesque attitudes and movements—reminded him of the painted clown whom he had seen last summer in the circus, and he laughed as he watched them" (102). Like McCarthy's Comanches appearing as painted clowns in a "death hilarious" (*Blood Meridian* 53), the soldiers are comic parodies of the human form. Bierce's scene unfolds with "hideous pantomime" as the wounded men desperately crawl like "great black beetles" (103). One of the men turns to the child with "a face that lacked a lower jaw—from the upper teeth to the throat was a great red gap fringed with hanging shreds of flesh and splinters of bone" giving him the "the appearance of a great bird of prey crimsoned in throat and breast by the blood of its quarry" (103). Wounded, man appears as a hideous comic absurdity, and the child's first reaction is to laugh at the spectacle. Uruburu finds Vernon Parrington's definition of naturalism in *Main Currents in American Thought* "closely related to the characteristics which define the American grotesque" since both dwell on physical and mental deformities (78).

Blood Meridian recites a litany of grotesque characters deformed by death or wounds. Although Toadvine's ears have been cut off, ironically he wears a necklace of ears; also one of his eyelids sags "where a knife had severed the small muscles" (87). Sproule's wounds fester and stink, and he awakes one night to find that a bat—with a "wrinkled pug face, small and vicious, bare lips crimped in a horrible smile"—has bitten him. His scream of "such outrage as to stitch a caesura in the pulsebeat of the world" does not elicit any sympathy from the kid, who spits and coolly responds, "I know your kind.... What's wrong with you is wrong all the way through," indicating his disdain for fear, as it is a sign of weakness (66).

The novel's pervasive grotesqueness is usually associated with the ubiquitous scenes of mindless violence. Everywhere McCarthy's landscapes are filled with corpses and geological signs of violence, and his cityscapes are no less chaotic. In the streets of Chihuahua, the prisoners are surrounded by the city's squalor:

> They passed ... maimed beggars sad-eyed in rags and children asleep in the shadows with flies walking their dreamless faces. Dark coppers in a clackdish, the shriveled eyes of the blind ... lepers moaning through the streets and naked dogs that seemed composed of bone entirely ... old women with faces dark and harrowed as the land squatting in the gutters.... Small orphans were abroad like irate dwarfs and fools and sots, drooling and flailing about ... where racks of guts hung black with flies and flayings of meat in great red sheets now darkened with the advancing day and the flensed and naked skulls of cows and sheep with their dull blue eyes glaring wildly and the stiff bodies of deer and javelina and ducks and quail and parrots, all wild things from the country round hanging head downward from hooks. (72–73)

In the town of Ures, the capital of Sonora, they encounter a "rabble unmatched for variety and sordidness" of "beggars and proctors of beggars and whores and pimps and vendors and filthy children and whole deputations of the blind and the maimed and the importunate all crying out" (200). Later in the night, after the gang's festivities, there is even more abject depravity:

> By midnight there were fires in the street and dancing and drunkenness and the house rang with the shrill cries of the whores and the rival packs of dogs had infiltrated the now partly darkened and smoking yard in the back where a vicious dogfight broke out over the charred racks of goatbones and where the first gunfire of the night erupted and wounded dogs howled and dragged themselves about until Glanton himself went out and killed them with his knife, a lurid scene in the flickering light, the wounded dogs silent save for the pop of their teeth, dragging themselves across the lot like seals or other things and crouching under the walls while Glanton walked them down and clove their skulls with the huge copperbacked beltknife. (202)

Death makes grotesque caricatures that terrify because of their awful, sublime realism. The grotesque image depends on fantastical horror, the "actual visible representations of our fears, guilts, and desires," opening the "subconscious channels, ordinarily locked, which keep us chained safely to our beliefs" (Uruburu 1).

Frank Norris helps define the American grotesque when he writes of the epic but absurd struggle between "strong-willed individuals" and the forces of nature and society (Uruburu 78). McCarthy's characters likewise suffer death while engaged in arrogant acts that have led them to fatal precipices. White Jackson, while still gloating over his supposed dominance over a lesser man and an inferior race, is suddenly beheaded by an avenging Black Jackson. His head rolls to Tobin's feet, yet his body, grotesquely, strangely, remains seated: "He was sat as before save headless, drenched in blood, the cigarillo still between his fingers, leaning toward the dark and smoking grotto in the flames where his life had gone" (107). In a swift application of natural law, Black Jackson proves him wrong, thereby subsuming White Jackson's racist argument of segregation to his own, superior truth of "survival of the fittest." Later in Tucson, Black Jackson again asserts his natural right to equality when he kills the belligerent Owens, the owner of a makeshift restaurant, who tries to deny him service because of his race. Likewise, the Comanches prove Captain White's racial arrogance to be inferior to their own, and the Yumas finally prove Glanton's gang wrong by easily massacring them after they let their guard down. In the judge's Darwinian world of natural rights, the final equation of any moral question is always solved by who survives.

Many of *Blood Meridian*'s characters illustrate the motif of arrogance leading to complacency—which, in a harsh environment, is always fatal. Naturalism creates the alpha male and alpha male contenders, but this genetic arrogance, warped by the big brain of human males, can push too far. What passes for courage usually places too much of a premium on free will over better judgment. As Terry Witek notes, the gang members lose their instinct for survival when they trade their nomadic plundering for the security of the ferry trade because they settle down, complacently, into a "domestic space" (141). For months the gang makes its living off party-raiding, plundering towns and Indian villages, and it is their ability to inhabit lawless spaces, to safely ride on out of towns after ransacking them, and to scalp along the trail, that allows them to continue on their "tether" of good fortune. When they stop too long, as they do at the Yuma River, their debauchery leads to carelessness. And in the naturalistic world of tooth and claw, every mistake entails a potentially deadly consequence.

The rise and fall of people's lives follows such predictable paths that many people have been led to believe they are part of a grand plan, predetermined by the universe or God. Perry Westbrook finds that determinism is "so much a part of naturalism" that the "terms are almost synonymous" (132). Naturalists envisage "man and his society as being in the clutch of natural forces, both interior and exterior," over which "only a limited control is possible" (132). The judge describes how "notions of chance and fate are the preoccupation of men engaged in rash undertakings" because the stakes are so high (*Blood Meridian* 153). In matters of life or death, men mostly prefer to believe in free will, since it elevates their own role in the universe to that of ruler. Of course, desperate men will sometimes hope that chance plays a part in the general order, especially if they are too weak to prevail except through good luck. Representing mankind's conceit, the judge baldly states, "Whatever in creation exists without my knowledge, exists without my consent" (198). Man wants to be free, to act of his own volition, to be "suzerain" of his own domain and his goal is always first to dream, then to create the dream, working it into existence. All "pockets of autonomous life" must be first sought out and discovered, or in the judge's vernacular "tabernacled," for autonomous life, even bits of it, can undo man's best laid plans. In the last three centuries since Bacon and the ensuing Age of Enlightenment, there have been unrelenting efforts to do exactly this. Every nook and cranny of the universe is being probed—from genes, viruses, bacteria, and atomic structure to stars, quasars, galaxies, and superclusters. It is in our nature to discover and catalog the farthest reaches of the universe since understanding may lead to control. Yet man is continually frustrated in the effort to control the universe, and in reaching for the stars, he often places himself in great danger. A false sense of control or incomplete knowledge can be an illusion that leads to complacency, which in a fatal environment can lead to annihilation.

At times the judge seems to suggest that truth and knowledge are attainable, as when he tells Toadvine, "That man who sets himself the task of singling out the thread of order from the tapestry will by the decision alone have taken charge of the world and it is only by such taking charge that he will effect a way to dictate the terms of his own fate" (199). And as the judge's victory dance implies, in the violent struggle of life, mankind can prevail. But individual triumphs are at best transitory. For in this story, despite our hopes to the contrary, man does not change destiny. Glanton's insane pact with the judge does not give him any extra time in the dance, while the kid, who does not meet the judge's criteria, survives longer than the others. But the fate of them all is to die violently, and the judge's malevolent victory dance is eternal only in its general application. His brag at the end that he "will never die" represents the brag of the whole species rather than of any one individual. His claim that certain true men will always dance is a universal truth, but the dancers keep changing since their particular time on the dance floor is finite. As a species we may well continue to outcompete all the other "bears," but each of us, one by one, will soon fail. The genetic and innate will to live and kill, savage and brutal, survives in us like a bad mutation, but individual free will is limited by time, chance, and perhaps even a malicious fate.

Glanton's men are not fearful, but they are desperate since they live for, and in, the moment, the *carpe diem,* whether in combat or revelry. At one point, Black Jackson wonders aloud if they will all "perish by the sword" as the Bible indicates (248). Ironically, the judge's exuberant free will, symbolized by his fiddling and nimble dancing, masks the paradox of man's double nature. Mankind's penchant for mindless violence and war prevents him from ever firmly grasping what he reaches for. The genetic violence of his left hand always destroys the civilized production of his right hand, and his quest for a better life becomes the paved road to mutual destruction. But perhaps we shouldn't dwell on such matters for too long. As Albert Camus has argued, man will always resist fate, and if it counters his right to exist, he can refuse to accept fate. However, as death is the one fate common to all men, the gang members sense that fortune-telling cannot be benign. The kid, Black Jackson, and Glanton are all wary and soon become angry during the reading of the tarot cards (95–96). And the judge himself, acting as a composite of Hobbes's First Man and Fukuyama's Last Man, certainly resists a malicious fate by destroying as much as he discovers, murdering as much as he saves. He is the double-column ledger book of human society itself, with every credit undone by a destructive debit, negating all efforts toward progress. The judge has no plans to pass on his journal to posterity, making the journal itself an image of fate, a book of life and death, as gang member Marcus Webster unconsciously realizes when he refuses to be drawn. The judge's own words reveal the nature of the book: "What is to be deviates no jot from the book wherein it's writ" (141). And the judge's known habit in the book of fate is to first record, or "tabernacle," every item he can find and, afterward, systematically to destroy it. Within the judge's book we find the story of man.

Like the gang members, we are usually too pleased with ourselves to long consider fate, since death is the ultimate fate subverting our best plans to live. McCarthy tells us in the first pages that the kid's origins are as "remote as is his destiny," yet he, like all men, will "try whether the stuff of creation may be shaped to man's will or whether his own heart is not another kind of clay" (4–5). McCarthy's theme of the will to live contravened by an apparently unfair fate takes an earlier naturalistic form in Stephen Crane's autobiographical story "The Open Boat," when four survivors of a shipwreck in a small dinghy woodenly mull over their chances of making it ashore:

> "If I am going to be drowned—if I am going to be drowned—if I am going to be drowned, why, in the name of the seven mad gods who rule the sea, was I allowed to come thus far and contemplate sand and trees?"
>
> During this dismal night, it may be remarked that a man would conclude that it was really the intention of the seven mad gods to drown him, despite the abominable injustice of it. For it was certainly an abominable injustice to drown a man who had worked so hard, so hard. The man felt it would be a crime most unnatural. Other people had drowned at sea since galleys swarmed with painted sails, but still—
>
> When it occurs to a man that nature does not regard him as important, and that she feels she would not maim the universe by disposing of him, he at first wishes to throw bricks at the temple, and he hates deeply the fact that there are no bricks and no temples. Any visible expression of nature would surely be pelleted with his jeers.
>
> Then, if there be no tangible thing to hoot, he feels, perhaps, the desire to confront a personification and indulge in pleas, bowed to one knee, and with hands supplicant, saying, "Yes, but I love myself."
>
> A high cold star on a winter's night is the word he feels that she says to him. Thereafter he knows the pathos of his situation. (*Complete Short Stories* 352–53)

The pathos of man's condition here is the result of realizing his powerlessness in the grip of nature's hand, of seeing, in a terrible instant, that he is not in control of his own life, and that no benevolent deities are apt to intervene. The impassive face of nature remains blank and stubbornly unpersonified, without sentience or any tangible evidence of metaphysics. The height and breadth of the universe, Crane's "high cold star," belittles not only one man but all of mankind and the small Earth he inhabits. Crane's luckless sailor is alone in the measureless immensity of water and sky and space, much as McCarthy's characters are alone under stars that burn with "lidless fixity" (213). Any personification of nature or of gods or metaphysics, according to the judge, is "the order in creation . . . which you have put there" (245). Naturalism's landscapes constantly remind readers of the harsh, uncaring nature of the universe. As the gang rides on through the desolation of the desert, they see dustspouts "wobbling and augered" and remember stories

> of pilgrims borne aloft like dervishes in those mindless coils to be dropped broken and bleeding upon the desert again and there perhaps to watch the thing that had destroyed them lurch onward like some drunken djinn and resolve itself once more into the elements from which it sprang. Out of that whirlwind no voice spoke and the pilgrim lying in his broken bones may cry out and in his anguish he may rage, but rage at what? And if the dried and blackened shell of him is found among the sands by travelers to come yet who can discover the engine of his ruin? (111)

While Crane's fatalism can, at times, approach that found in the Greek tradition of heroic tragedy, in which the narrator laments his fate and faces death with stoic fatalism, nowhere in *Blood Meridian* can such sentiments be evoked in the meager articulation of its characters' grunts and spits. McCarthy's apelike men do not get much chance to contemplate as death quickly overtakes them.

When the judge performs his preternatural coin trick, tossing it playfully into space, the men watch it orbit the campfire and return to the judge's hand. Then the coin is thrown far into the night and is gone for quite a while, only to return "with a faint high droning" and a "light slap" into the judge's outstretched hand. He informs his audience that "Moons, coins, men" are all alike in forming an "arc of circling bodies" on a tether (245–46). It is a prescient demonstration of destiny, which is always as certain as gravity. The lives of men exist no longer in the universe than the flight of the coin, and the judge, or one whom he knows well, holds the tether (328). The kid's tether is just a little longer than those of the rest of the gang, by about twenty-nine years, until the judge's outstretched hands finally reach for his life in the jakes of Fort Griffin.

The final lecture of the judge in Fort Griffin's bar, delivered to the kid now grown into "the man," reiterates much of the novel's philosophical ground, summarizing McCarthy's thematic positions on the existence of fate and chance, men's place in a violent, uncaring universe, and the man's failure to fully enter the warrior's victory dance. Although the man is uninterested, as always, in the judge's rambling erudition and insists on answering his queries with the usual snorts and grunts, the judge continues lecturing him on the infallibility of his own fate. He gestures to the people, proclaiming, "Order is not set aside because of their indifference" (328). He warns obscurely that the evening encounter is an "orchestration for an event" and that the "participants will be apprised of their roles at the proper time" (328–29). Pointing to another man in the room, apparently as a random example, the judge assesses mankind's false sense of control and free will:

> Yet his complaint that a man's life is no bargain masks the actual case with him. Which is that men will not do as he wishes them to. Have never done, never will do. That's the way of things with him and his life is so balked about by difficulty and become so altered of its intended architecture that he is little more than a walking hovel hardly fit to house the human spirit at all. Can he say, such a man, that there is no malign thing set against him? That there is no power and no force and no cause? What manner of heretic could doubt agency and claimant alike? Can he believe that the wreckage of his existence is unentailed? No liens, no creditors? That gods of vengeance and of compassion alike lie sleeping in their crypt and whether our cries are for an accounting or for the destruction of the ledgers altogether they must evoke only the same silence and that it is this silence which will prevail? (330)

Here the judge echoes Crane's comment about the apparent obdurate malevolence of the "seven mad gods" and the silent witness of the "high cold star." The judge tells the man that the figurative desert of man's fate is "ultimately empty. It is hard, it is barren. Its very nature is stone" (*Blood Meridian* 330). The man's reaction, as always, is a wary, yet ignorant, dismissal.

James Dickey is perhaps the best example of another contemporary southern writer who, like McCarthy, relies on the traditions of literary naturalism. All of its conventions operate in his poems and stories; both his novels, *Deliverance* and *To the White Sea,* show man's atavistic instinct to survive when confronted with a hostile environment. In *Babel to Byzantium,* Dickey describes his own work as a search for the "animal grace of human beings," which, like Hemingway's work, is revealed in the lives of soldiers, hunters, and athletes (291–92). These roles call for ancient instincts and reduce moral complexities to the simple binary relationship of predator and prey. In *Deliverance,* the Appalachian backwoods are as "wild as Alaska" (4), and the suburban protagonists must discover their own potential as hunters/warriors and develop as well a "sense of understanding with the hunted animal" (*Babel* 292). Competition and fatal environments give Dickey's characters opportunities to reveal "grace under pressure." It is naturalism combined with the tragic hero and romanticism's sublime beauty. In *To the White Sea,* a downed pilot learns to fight his way north, killing as necessary. Like Crane's narrator in "Open Boat," Dickey's characters are "battling against universal dissolution, . . . the loss of all he and other men have been given as human beings, of all they have loved and been moved by" (*Babel* 281).

In depicting violent contests, there is a fine distinction at times between historical romance and historical nightmare. The truths McCarthy has to tell are part of the American grotesque, most fully developed in naturalism and intensified by postmodernism. The absurd ironies of *Blood Meridian* are not those of Thomas Berger's *Little Big Man* or the New Western History's revisionism. *Blood Meridian* contains these truths but moves beyond them to a simpler, darker, older truth: mankind is a natural-born killer. If the "pure products of America go crazy," as William Carlos Williams said, that is because they are purely human. We are atavistic, contagious, and random, children of a violent, mindless universe. What disturbs Peter Josyph most about *Blood Meridian* is what disturbs us all—the judge, leering, smiling, pontificating, bragging, infantile, naked, perverse. He is a demented embodiment of Walt Whitman, who celebrates himself "for good or bad," weaving the joyous exuberant song of himself, "hankering, gross, mystical, nude" ("Song of Myself," line 389):

> I know I am deathless,
> I know this orbit of mine cannot be swept by a carpenter's compass,
> I know I shall not pass like a child's carlacue cut with a burnt stick at night.
> I know I am August,
> I do not trouble my spirit to vindicate itself or be understood,
> I see that the elementary laws never apologize,
> (I reckon I behave no prouder than the level I plant my house by, after all.)
> I exist as I am, that is enough.
>
> ("Song of Myself," lines 406–13)

Whereas Whitman's "barbaric yawp" extols the virtues of the American empire—diverse, democratic, full of possibility—Judge Holden is the poet of death. He, more than the kid, represents the ultimate child with "a taste for mindless violence. All history present in that visage" (3). He is the mad, murdering god Lucifer, Yahweh, Shiva, a gentleman and fraud, an eternal form of mankind, well versed in all philosophy, multilingual yet still naked, bestial, crouching, sweating by a campfire. He is Last and First Man. There is no David to stand up to this Goliath. The kid cannot articulate, cannot defend, civilized moral sensibilities; he does not develop into a man capable of understanding the judge. We have to pitch in to save ourselves. Indeed, this is what bothers us so much. We are in danger from this text. It is our own part in the awful "orchestration of events" we worry about. We want mystery, religion, compassion, cooperation, and democratic freedom. Our much-vaunted American dream of progress is being "pitched off down the rocks into the abyss below" (195), shattered and lost in the novel's "shoreless void" (246). As Paul Civello suggests, naturalism in a postmodern context is nothing less than "the collapse... of humanity's conception of an order in the material world" (124). McCarthy forces us to witness too much—the plain evidence of ruins, of corpses, of vanished seas, of "stones and trees, the bones of things."

Four

Western Myths in *All the Pretty Horses* and *The Crossing*

> There isn't a place in the world you can go where they don't know about cowboys and Indians and the myth of the West.
> —Cormac McCarthy

The Border Trilogy avoids many of the unsettling questions posed in *Blood Meridian,* although both John Grady Cole and Billy Parham are like the kid in one respect: they find unexpected dangers in Mexico. Like the kid, the protagonists of *All the Pretty Horses* and *The Crossing* are nomadic, aggressive, independent, and lucky in surviving potentially fatal encounters. While all three stories provide the necessary tests for traditional rites of initiation and share structural characteristics with the bildungsroman, the kid of *Blood Meridian* does not achieve maturity or awareness, or experience life-changing moments of existential glory. And in the end, he dies ignominiously. In contrast, John Grady and Billy pass through their tests with transcendent moments of honor, becoming experienced in the ways of the world.

The first two novels in the Border Trilogy represent a mythic fault line in McCarthy's career. For one thing, the cowboy protagonists are likable, good-natured young men who set off on quests for adventure, in the mode of Huck Finn. Unlike the kid of *Blood Meridian,* the protagonists of the Border Trilogy are fully developed, three-dimensional characters assuming mythic roles in familiar western narratives. Although the ruthless, violent intensity of McCarthy's former novels is gone, there are, of course, many stylistic parallels found in the Border novels. McCarthy's signature prose is still recognizable in four distinctive patterns: metaphysical canticle; expansive, poetic narrative; terse, minimal realism; and the use of Spanish. In *Blood Meridian,* the metaphysical canticle can be heard in the philosophical rantings of the judge, who preaches the historical theology of violence. In *All the Pretty Horses* and *The Crossing,* the metaphysical canticle is used in the monologues of numerous old anchorites, such as Dueña Alfonsa's speech comparing the fates of nations and individuals (*All the Pretty Horses* 229–40). Expansive, poetic narrative, used so often for surrealistic descriptions in *Blood Meridian,* is still present in landscape passages, although it now evokes nostalgic beauty and tragic loss instead of developing *Blood Meridian*'s theme of mindless violence. (As we shall see in the next chapter, McCarthy packs various motifs into his richly textured narratives, using imagistic language to double and foreshadow events.) As in earlier novels, McCarthy again relies on his distinctive unpunctuated minimal realism for the quick-moving dramatic freight of dialogue and action. This minimalism, reminiscent of Hemingway and Raymond Carver, creates a close-to-the-bone cinematic clarity. The understated, ungrammatical lingo of the cowboys also leads to moments of wry comic repartee. And Spanish is even more prevalent throughout the Border Trilogy, sending non-Spanish-speaking readers rushing to their dictionaries for translations. Despite the frequency of bilingual passages, the Border Trilogy remains predicated upon a very Anglo point of view. Unlike Latino writers such as Rudolfo Anaya and Gloria Anzaldúa, who use bilingual codeswitching as part of the narrative voice, McCarthy employs Spanish to authenticate his locale, imparting a realistic sense of the borderlands. Like the ever-present tortillas and eggs, the Spanish adds a necessary detail to the fictional milieu. All of McCarthy's western novels remain solidly fixed on white male experiences, as no Mexican characters ever step forward to become integral members of the main storylines. Rather, the Mexicans are left on the periphery in supporting roles. One telling detail, perhaps, is found in *All the Pretty Horses*: Alejandra's blue eyes and her fluency in English. Her wealthy, European roots are emphasized over her Indian ancestry. Alejandra's white ethnicity develops the novel's underlying myth of American progress, a conservative, ethnocentric myth based on Anglo-American superiority and entitlement. Her whiteness matches a white heroine to a white hero.

Throughout the Border Trilogy, McCarthy's thematic treatment of western myth is complicated by the setting. The protagonists seek adventure not by going out west but by going south into Mexico. This left turn across the border traditionally has been a wrong move for the American cowboy. Unlike the West, which Anglo-Americans assumed from early on extended from "sea to shining sea," Old Mexico has always been viewed as a badlands, an empty space, a rough place of bandits and criminals and the evil, foreign Other. It is a place beyond the pale of American law. After the War with Mexico and the Gadsden Purchase, which resulted in significant new territory, including Texas, New Mexico, Arizona, and California, Americans mostly left Mexico to the Apaches and Mexicans. Although the Texas Rangers crossed on occasion in pursuit of Anglo-American interests, and the shifting sands of the Rio Grande resulted in many minor disputes, Mexico has mostly been ignored until recently, except during the Revolution and Pancho Villa's subsequent raid on Columbus, New Mexico, in 1916. Mexico is a foreign place where American heroics clash with, and are thwarted by, cultural differences. Nevertheless, McCarthy's young protagonists stubbornly venture south in search of the Old West that they can no longer find in the western United States. The western frontier is gone, declared closed, moved north to Alaska or overseas to Asia. American law and government hold sway over all United States soil. To find frontier adventures, McCarthy's cowboys have only one choice.

The women who populate McCarthy's westerns remain in domestic roles as thoroughly stolid mothers and wives who fix meals for the ravenous boys and help nurse them back to health. As heroines, McCarthy's females are underdeveloped, two-dimensional figures kept off to the side. They do not take center stage; we do not hear much about their innermost fears and desires. We are not really given much about them beyond their immediate function in relation to the boys. Throughout the first two novels of the Border Trilogy, the protagonists' love interests are ephemeral and serve mostly as tragic markers along the trail to manhood. Generally speaking, in a male rite-of-passage myth, romance does not lead to domestic stability. Girls represent femmes fatales as idealized sexual objects, who, ultimately, are unattainable. In such stories, the romantic heroes must ride away alone, sadder but wiser for their experiences. I anticipate that some critics will find McCarthy's mythic West in the Border Trilogy full of the old racist and sexist stereotypes seen so often in western films and novels. Like Larry McMurtry, McCarthy pursues a very Anglo-male trail, playing to the common ethos of a cowboy-loving crowd. Without altering basic mythic types or classic plots, he plays with poetic language and thematic motifs.

In *All the Pretty Horses* and *The Crossing* we notice the reiteration of familiar words from McCarthy's stock diction: *cold, pale, gray, void, vault, blood, red, moon, sun,* as well as *Blood Meridian*'s famous scene-changing curtain line, "they rode on." Visual motifs often begin with the characters sitting around a campfire and typically sweep upward from the sparks into the black void of sparklike stars, a move that provides McCarthy ample opportunities for intertextual motifs and doubling. One such reference occurs in the beginning of *All the Pretty Horses*: "The night was cold and clear and the sparks rising from the fire raced hot and red among the stars" (9–10). The cinematic visual effect, from campfire to stars, emphasizes mankind's primal beginnings and his remote isolation in the vast cosmos.

Unlike *Blood Meridian,* the Border Trilogy places McCarthy squarely in the hoary tradition of purple sage romances. The narrative platforms of these novels are constructed on two frontier paradigms: the progress myth and the primitive-pastoral myth. *All the Pretty Horses* retells the myth of American progress, whereas *The Crossing* plays out the primitive-pastoral myth. Both stories center around young romantic heroes of the type R.W.B. Lewis has named "the American Adam."[1] The heroic protagonists of the Border Trilogy have many of the characteristics of the Adamic icon found throughout American fiction from James Fenimore Cooper to Norman Mailer. Lewis's definitive study, *The American Adam,* (1955) describes this traditional character as an "an individual standing alone, self-reliant and self-propelling, ready to confront whatever awaited him with the aid of his own unique and inherent resources" (5). In the progress myth, the young American Adam represents our national hopes for the future as he battles the foreign Other in defense of Anglo-American dreams. In him, within one character, all the hopes of progress combine with the vagrancies of youth. Torn away from a domestic Edenic sanctuary, an American Adam strikes out alone with naïve, impossible dreams. In the wilderness he faces challenges, living in the present, without much forethought about danger or failure. The wilderness can serve as various symbolic places. In a primitive-pastoral myth, the hero discovers paradise in the wilderness. Other times, the wilderness becomes a purgatory of loneliness, in which the primitive hero must purge his soul and ready himself for mythic battle.

But in all of his manifestations, the young American Adam is unabashedly heroic. Like most teenagers living on the stuff of dreams, he leaps for existential highs and often enough finds himself on uncertain ground. He thrives on challenges, confronts authority, follows his heart, and gorges on life. Exuberance and a romantic impulse are an American Adam's chief strengths. In the first two novels of the Border Trilogy, bingeing on eggs and tortillas becomes a gustatory motif for youthful overindulgence, a satiation of the sensual. Oftentimes romantic impulses serve the protagonist well, especially in competitive or dangerous situations. But in affairs of the heart, they ultimately prove to be his undoing. For the sin of an American Adam is like the original: he dares to choose Eve over God. His sin, too, is sexual.

In these westerns God appears as various authority figures who enforce the rules of society. As in oral traditions, in fictional retellings there is much room for straying from the original myth. The American Adam is involved with Eve and, because of his defiance, loses paradise. However, not every detail of an Adamic narrative need fit the pattern of the Book of Genesis. In McCarthy's versions, Eden is embodied as the idyllic dream. For John Grady, Eden is found in a cowboy's paradise, whereas Billy searches for it with wolf in tow, up in the high-mountain wilderness of the Pilares. McCarthy's narratives contain no external serpents. Rather, his Adamic figures are tempted by their own willful dreams; they dare to pit themselves against the conventions of society. It is the sin of Lucifer. They presume to cross the border and to act according to their own volition. They go to Mexico on the flimsiest of pretexts: to retrieve stolen horses, to relocate a wolf, to find a lost brother. Examining the Adamic hero in the works of Melville, R.W.B. Lewis notes that the Adamic hero, "going forth toward experience, the inventor of his own character ... is made to confront that 'other'—the world or society" (111). In the inevitable fall from grace, the rebel Adam matures in "perception and moral intelligence" so that the forbidden fruit—whatever form it may take—becomes a catalyst for obtaining worldly knowledge (Lewis 127). The narrative of the American Adam, therefore, becomes a rite of initiation. In this paradigm, the fall of Adam is an inevitable loss of innocence—an induction into a world of men. The hard lessons come not only via the tree of knowledge (or experience) but from the loss of the dream garden.

In both the progress and primitive-pastoral myths, the young Adamic hero is fated to lose the domestic comforts of society. In the progress myth, the hero saves Anglo society from the evil foreign oppressor and is recognized for his valor, whereas in the primitive-pastoral myth, the hero remains a lonely wanderer as an outcast. Both kinds of heroes find glory and redemption in the fight against the oppressive authority of society. The primary difference between the two types is that the progress hero seeks redemption by fighting for Anglo-American interests while the primitive-pastoral hero seeks redemption by fighting against oppressive authority and rejecting domesticity.

Americans have consistently perpetuated two frontier myths, one that champions progress and Anglo-American might and one that champions the preservation of wilderness and its idealized natives. The new world was thus viewed as two very different places: a hostile desert place full of the barbarous enemy or a pastoral Edenic garden full of idyllic innocents. Both of these ideological antipodes drew Europeans west. Today, in our modern society of cities and suburbs with our myriad "promises to keep"—the obligations to family and employer, to community and church—the primitive-pastoral act of breaking free to "light out for the Territory" still resonates. Yet the two dreams are very different. The dream of progress—holding down a job, buying a house, raising a family—fulfills the promise of the American frontier: pioneering a homestead and building a domestic paradise log by log. But, paradoxically, after this dream of progress is attained, Americans may secretly bemoan their loss of inspiration, their yearning for a pastoral "white goddess" in Robert Graves's term, a muse of individuality. Thus besieged, the typical suburbanite may gnash his teeth on the same old daily bread. Encumbered by marriage and family and job, the commuter may yearn for the mythic freedom and individualism of the Old West, the pristine beauty of a wilderness. He may rebel, perhaps in small ways, taking off from work a bit early on a sunny afternoon and playing a round of golf on company time. Or he might read a good old-fashioned western.

At the height of his existential glory, flinging off the traditional and conservative, a primitive-pastoral American Adam defies authority and rebels. For this act, he is, of course, promptly thrown out of the garden. In elevating his own character above society, the primitive hero loses against the more powerful social forces: family, business, church, and government. As an outlaw, he pursues romantic dreams originating in innocent, nonviolent pastoralism. But the exigencies of his confrontation with authority soon place him in combative scenarios. In his radical quest for individual freedom, the primitive-pastoral hero stumbles into issues larger than his own dreams. In some versions he may be converted to a cause, perhaps deciding to help fight for the preservation of his wilderness paradise. The primitive-pastoral hero thus defies the machine of progress, which would destroy the wilderness. He sheds his innocence for militancy, a warrior's stoicism. After a struggle, the primitive-pastoral hero may survive to wander alone, an ascetic, isolated from all domestic comforts in a society he has eschewed. D. H. Lawrence saw the primitive-pastoral hero as "the American male in retreat from civilization" (Love 198). Critic David Noble notes that an American Adam can form no permanent relationship with Eve (14). Adam's love for Eve is sinful because it intrudes upon his love for God. The tragedy of the American Adam is not so much his fall from grace, which is considered a triumphant rebellion against oppressive authority, as his loss of Eve's love. For outside the domesticity of the dream garden, there can be no Eve. The failure of the dream precludes any long-lasting union. After his moment of glorious rebellion and inevitable fall, the American Adam is alone, left with the unforeseen consequences of his actions.

William Faulkner's classic story "The Bear" portrays this theme well and is clearly McCarthy's literary antecedent for the section of *The Crossing* that could be titled "The Wolf." In the conventional primitive-pastoral plot of "The Bear," Ike McCaslin, a young man on the cusp of manhood, is presented with a chance to join the men of his Anglo-American society by hunting and killing the symbol of nature, the bear. This young hero finds moments of epiphany in which he discovers a primitive-pastoral identity that confronts his heritage as plantation owner. In his quest for the bear, the boy finds a life that allows him to live honestly, without the shame of a slaveholding past. At first Ike sets out to kill the bear, a deity of nature that wreaks enough perennial havoc on nearby farmers that it has come to personify all of the hated aspects of an untamed wilderness. From his half-Indian mentor, Boon, Ike learns that the only way to approach this preternatural animal is to leave behind the implements and weapons of civilization and to approach it unarmed. Through Boon's tutelage, the boy encounters the mysterious bear several times and comes to respect it as a living embodiment of the wilderness. The bear quest transforms the boy into a man who empathizes with his quarry more than with the hunters. Although the bear is eventually killed by the persistence of Boon and his half-wild dog, Ike becomes aware of the unethical bargain his ancestors made in acquiring the plantation, and he makes the moral decision to repudiate his birthright and its corrupting wealth. Primitive-pastoral experiences in the wilderness give him the requisite perspective to see the immorality of Southern society. Ike chooses instead a more Christlike role, working with his hands as a common carpenter.

Old Mexico serves as a primitive setting where boys may be tested by wilderness experiences. By turning south, the protagonists are turning back history to the frontier conditions of the Old West. In setting his westerns in Mexico, McCarthy follows Bharati Mukherjee's advice to "make the familiar exotic, and the exotic familiar" (Moyers). Although Mexico adjoins America's West, in many ways it might as well be another continent, given its mixture of Spanish and Indian languages, its differing tribes and ethnic *mestizo,* and the blending of Catholic with Native religions. McCarthy's liberal dollops of Spanish add an exotic linguistic component. The Mexican locale allows McCarthy ample opportunity to invoke his favorite Catholic motifs, including a litany of destroyed churches, ex-priests, and destitute pilgrims. Religious ideals prove no more permanent or resistant to ruin than any other idealistic dream.

Throughout the Border Trilogy, dreams of all kinds are destroyed by the chaos of the Mexican Revolution.

In *All the Pretty Horses,* John Grady's dream quest for manhood is prompted by a flurry of disappointments, beginning with his grandfather's death. The ranch, his hope for the future, is suddenly taken from him. His father, already divorced from his mother, and thus also divorced from any legal right to the ranch, has not been around much to teach him the lessons of life. His absent father has formed no lasting ties or emotional bonds, and he has no meaningful philosophy to pass on. He is a drifter who relies on café humor and reads the newspaper for small entertainments, such as the trivial news about Shirley Temple's divorce. He admits, "I aint no freethinker, but I'll tell you what. I'm a long way from bein convinced that [life's] all that good a thing" (13). Loneliness sets in as the boy goes into town at night to look up at the hotel room where "[his] father's shadow would pass behind the gauzy window curtains" (15). The last few days spent riding horses with his father only confirm that there is nothing more to learn from that source. His father is in the thrall of terminal disease and sees no purpose and no future in the landscape, which to him has only been "made suspect by what he'd seen of it elsewhere" (23).

His mother has her own glamorous dreams of the stage and city life, and as a result, cares little for the dreams of her son. One night at the dinner table, she abruptly dismisses his idea of taking over the ranch, belittling it as juvenile: "You're being ridiculous. You have to go to school" (15). John Grady is left sitting under the "picturebook" horses, which represent the mythic dream of the wilderness and its heroic possibilities. Dianne Luce interprets the allusion of the book's title to the nursery rhyme as part of the "child's natural sense of entitlement":

Hushaby,
Don't you cry,
Go to sleepy, little baby,
When you wake,
You shall have,
All the pretty little horses—
Blacks and bays,

> Dapples and grays,
> Coach and six-a little horses.
> (Luce 156)

In *All the Pretty Horses,* John Grady will return to his love of horses, as they prove more reliable and less complicated than other dreams. His love for horses marks him as a traditional cowboy hero, in love with the cowboy's wandering, rustic life.

Before his journey into Mexico, John Grady is unsure of what he is to become. At one of his mother's plays, he watches with "great intensity" to see if perhaps her art can teach him about life but instead learns, "There was nothing in it at all" (21). As he waits for her in the Menger Hotel, she rushes by him with a "man in a suit and a topcoat" (22). With the death of his grandfather, John Grady has lost the only role model he ever really had. To complete his separation from all domestic ties, he even loses his girlfriend to a more modern rival who owns a car. There are no hopes left for a future in this place, nothing to keep John Grady from leaving to find something better. Despite his father's and mother's inattention, John Grady does have the memory of a heroic grandfather—a survivor, the last of eight sons—who carved out a life for himself on the ranch. He is like the grandfather from John Steinbeck's classic story "The Leader of the People," who tells stories of pioneering: "It was westering and westering. Every man wanted something for himself, but the big beast that was all of them wanted only westering" (414). In Steinbeck's story the grandson lies awake at night dreaming of his grandfather "on a huge white horse, marshaling the people," envisioning the pioneers as a "race of giants . . . fearless men, men of a staunchness unknown in this day" (410). John Grady is also an heir apparent to that dreamy mythic life, a future now suddenly wide open with the possibilities of a saddle and beautiful, strong horses—horses, however, that his grandfather reminded him exist only in a "picturebook" (16).

Unlike the nineteenth-century American Adam, whom Lewis defines as being "unfettered from his past," the modern Adam must confront the daunting heritage of his western forebears. If the first pioneers were free to define themselves and to create their own will, to carve out their own mythic space, the modern western hero, in contrast, is firmly rooted in the history and legends of his forefathers. For John Grady, the stories of his pioneering grandfather are a source of inspiration and a high-water mark for him to equal. The long rides with his father only confirm that his destiny is in the saddle, which also happens to be the only literal inheritance from his father. The journey that horses offer him will be his only chance at matching the grandfather's ancestral heritage:

> The boy who rode on slightly before him sat a horse not only as if he'd been born to it which he was but as if were he begot by malice or mischance into some queer land where horses never were he would have found them anyway. Would have known that there was something missing for the world to be right or he right in it and would have set forth to wander wherever it was needed for as long as it took until he came upon one and he would have known that that was what he sought and it would have been. (23)

Horses represent his hope for a meaningful life, the life of the "ardenthearted," with all "the blood and the heat of the blood that ran them" (6), the life of his grandfather who pioneered Comanche country. The landscape of *Blood Meridian*'s Old West is briefly evoked when John Grady rides down the "old Comanche road" where "you could see the faint trace of it bearing south" and the "sun sat blood red and elliptic under the reefs of bloodred cloud before him" (5). His father also observes, "We're like the Comanches was two hundred years ago." (25–26). Both father and son yearn for a better life, but his father's chance at it has already passed, and for John Grady a better life is no longer possible in this place. The "faint trace" of the Comanche road beckons him south, into Mexico. The scene has been set for a traditional American drama of a boy's dream quest, seeking adventure and manhood in a heroic past.

In *Cruising Paradise* (1996), Sam Shepard explores the same thematic territory by looking past his father back to older, heroic roots. His label for the American Adam is "The Self-Made Man," and he unearths examples of him among the old family albums, finding the evidence of him in the "hard-set jawline" of his ancestors, "men with long beards and wide-brimmed straw hats, standing three abreast atop giant hay wagons, wooden pitchforks in hand, almost biblical against the prairie sky. Railroad men riding cowcatchers, waving derbies; blasting their way through granite mountains; unstoppable in their absolute conviction of Manifest Destiny" (3). He lingers on the photograph of his grandfather, hoping to find his own jawline in the old photograph. Outside in the night, he senses the overwhelming presence of loneliness, which he has come to accept and trust more than the comfort of a woman since he knows the night will always be there. Shepard's autobiographical protagonist seeks his heritage in the loneliness of the open road and vast emptiness of western landscapes. Like McCarthy's characters, he receives no guidance from his father and grows up to wander the West, crossing the border at times in his search for adventure.

In *The Crossing,* Billy's venture into Mexico also begins with a sense of dissatisfaction with his present circumstances. Instead of a quest for picturebook horses and old Comanche trails, Billy's dreams involve wolves. Alone one winter's night, he encounters the surreal vision of a wolf pack:

> They were running on the plain harrying the antelope and the antelope moved like phantoms in the snow and circled and wheeled and the dry powder blew about them in the cold moonlight and their breath smoked palely in the cold as if they burned with some inner fire and the wolves twisted and turned and leapt in a silence such that they seemed of another world entire. They moved down the valley and turned and moved far out on the plain until they were the smallest of figures in that dim whiteness and then they disappeared. (4)

It is a transfiguring moment of epiphany for Billy. Stronger than any domestic tie with his parents, he feels the "call of the wild" in the mountains. McCarthy has used wolves before to symbolize the wilderness. In *Blood Meridian* wolves trail along behind Glanton's gang, forming a double of the men, and the two bands seem like natural counterparts. John Sepich, noting thirty-two references to wolves in the text, suggests that they may be "emblematic of the non-moral rapacity" of mankind (145). At one point, Tobin tells the kid, "I would never shoot a wolf and I know other men of the same sentiments" (*Blood Meridian* 129). Squatters and farmers hate wolves and kill them as they would thieves, but upon hearing the howling of a solitary wolf, the "hunters smiled among themselves" (117). Judge Holden's comment that "wolves cull themselves, man" (146) supports his theory that man is at heart wild and menacing like the wolf, and that the natural law demanding survival of the fittest extends to his own species.

In *Of Wolves and Men,* Barry Lopez describes the close affinity between wolves and primitive man. In the earliest art of the Lascaux caves in France, wolves are shown stalking game (96). Throughout European history the wolf has assumed various guises: the patron of warriors, the devil, an allegorical representation of savagery or greed. Myths of wolves have evolved into the familiar tales of werewolves preying on children (Lopez 204–8). Wolves are shadow creatures, rarely sighted except during the twilight hours of dusk or dawn. They have always been heard more than seen, terrifying men who huddled at night in the safety of campfires. Wolves rule the night and wilderness, and only men who are like wolves themselves dare venture into the night. Lopez notes that man's chief rival for hunting and territory has always been the wolf pack. Men and wolves share the ancient bond of hunting the same prey, with one often eating the kills of the other. Many native tribes have placed the wolf at the center of their mythic universe, donning their skins and masks in holy ceremonies as well as in the hunt itself (96). White settlers often equated wolves with Indians and sought to destroy both. Lopez sees the nineteenth- and twentieth-century destruction of wolves as part of the westward movement:

> This twined sense of wilderness as a place innately dangerous and godless was something that attached itself, inevitably, to the wolf—the most feared denizen of gloomy wilderness. As civilized man matured and came to measure his own progress by his subjugation of the wilderness—both clearing trees for farms and clearing pagan minds for Christian ideas—the act of killing wolves became a symbolic act, a way to lash out at that enormous, inchoate obstacle: wilderness. (141)

Paradoxically, wolves and men are very much alike. Wolves and wild dogs were easy to domesticate since early man likewise shared the thrill of the hunt and affinity for life in bands. Like Lopez, McCarthy has been attracted to wolves; he was reportedly involved in discussions with Edward Abbey about a "covert operation to reintroduce the wolf to southern

Arizona" (Woodward 30). By giving Billy a wolf identity, McCarthy injects all of these historical and symbolic meanings into the novel's primitive-pastoral theme.

In *The Crossing,* Billy's own Comanche road back to the wilderness of yesteryear is symbolized by an old Indian whom he and his brother discover near a waterhole. *Blood Meridian* is briefly echoed in the image of the sun, which "simmered in a dry red lake under the barren mountains" (*The Crossing* 5) and in the sunset: "the western sky was a deep red under the reefs of cloud" (8). The old Indian's eyes mesmerize Billy: "Eyes so dark they seemed all pupil. Eyes in which the sun was setting. In which the child stood beside the sun" (5–6). McCarthy extends and develops the moment with an expansive description of eyes and suns and destiny:

> He had not known that you could see yourself in others' eyes nor see therein such things as suns. He stood twinned in those dark wells with hair so pale, so thin and strange, the selfsame child. As if it were some cognate child to him that had been lost who now stood windowed away in another world where the red sun sank eternally. As if it were a maze where these orphans of his heart had miswandered in their journey in life and so arrived at last beyond the wall of that antique gaze from whence there could be no way back forever. (6)

McCarthy's penchant for intertextual motifs and fantastical, surreal images is evident in this passage, in which the child of nature, the Old West, and the red sun sinking eternally converge in the eyes of Billy to form a shared destiny. Time has come to a standstill; it crosses paths with the Old West in an otherworldly conjunction of characters. Like the kid of *Blood Meridian,* this boy of fourteen will also have to leave home and find his future in the wilderness. John Grady and Billy both embark on journeys of self-discovery to find an acceptable manhood that binds them to an ancestral past where Indians, horses, and wolves signify a noble savagery.

Unlike any of McCarthy's other novels, *The Crossing* really has three beginnings: one in which Billy captures the wolf and begins a dream quest to take it back to the high mountains of Mexico; a second one in which Billy and Boyd set out to find adventure after the death of their parents; and a third one in Billy's journey back to Mexico to find Boyd. In the second departure for Mexico, Billy and Boyd go in search of stolen horses, which recalls the journey in *All the Pretty Horses*. Like John Grady, Billy and Boyd have nothing left to keep them in town. Their parents have been killed, and they are too young to be allowed to work the ranch. They are drawn south to restore what is rightfully theirs and thus find a balance on their own scales of justice. It is a wildly improbable scheme to retrieve the stolen horses, but out of such is the stuff of picturebook dreams.

In *All the Pretty Horses*, after John Grady and Rawlins join up with Jimmy Blevins, they ride up into the mountains, leaving civilization behind. When Rawlins asks, "Where do you reckon that paradise is at?" (59) it is the right question for an American Adam. That night the howl of a lone wolf, which the boys hear before they fall asleep, is the signal that they have arrived in the primitive-pastoral wilderness. John Grady watches the stars "while he contemplated the wildness about him, the wildness within" (60). The boys forage and hunt as they live off the land, eating a jackrabbit that Blevins has shot. The natives likewise appear increasingly primitive, like "small ragged caravans of migrant traders" with their handmade rope and "packframes made from treelimbs" (65).

Blevins soon becomes a point of contention between Rawlins and John Grady. Rawlins wants to ditch Blevins as soon as possible since he recognizes the danger of riding with such an unpredictable person. Blevins and Rawlins represent two opposing forces vying for control of John Grady's will. Rawlins is the practical voice of reason, calling on John Grady to retreat from idealistic principles and submit to reality, while Blevins is the wild shout of unbridled idealism. Rawlins tells John Grady at one point, "A goodlookin horse is like a goodlookin woman. . . . They're always more trouble than what they're worth. What a man needs is just one that will get the job done" (89). John Grady, however, persistently refuses to believe that reality is a force to be reckoned with. He prefers a beautiful girl just as he prefers picturebook horses. Rawlins and Blevins represent pragmatism versus idealism, facts versus dreams, and John Grady has heard enough of the voice of reason before, from his mother and the lawyer. If he had listened to it then, he would not even be in Mexico. It is a voice he will later hear from Dueña Alfonsa warning him to stay away from Alejandra when she tells him quite correctly: "In the end we all come to be cured of our sentiments. Those whom life does not cure death will. The world is quite ruthless in selecting between the dream and the reality, even where we will not" (238). But as an American Adam, John Grady will always reach for the forbidden fruit, and thus he sympathizes with the extreme romantic sensibility of Blevins rather than the dull reality of Rawlins. John Grady admires Blevins's dead-center shot through Rawlins's wallet, which validates him as more than a simpleminded braggart. He becomes a legendary character, a dead-eye shot right out of Buffalo Bill's Wild West Show, which Rawlins sarcastically alludes to when he asks, "You ready, Annie Oakley?" (48). Blevins's determination and impractical idealism engage John Grady's own sense of adventure. Paradoxically, it is the flaw that ennobles yet destroys. In sharing a romantic, rebellious sensibility, Blevins and John Grady find that their greatest strength is also their Adamic sin. To act on picturebook dreams means disregarding the solid realities of social conventions.

Early on, Rawlins correctly identifies Blevins as the source of their future troubles. After the storm in which Blevins drunkenly claims to be a human lightning rod, Rawlins suggests they just leave him. John Grady, however, argues for compassion. Rawlins clearly sees the futility of trying to recover Blevins's lost horse, while John Grady naively insists, "It aint goin to hurt us to try and help the boy get his horse back" (74). In town, when they spot the horse and decide what to do, Rawlins warns: "Ever dumb thing I ever done in my life there was a decision I made before that got me into it. It was never the dumb thing. It was always some choice I'd made before it" (79). This is to be the first of several tests of John Grady's grace under pressure, and like Hemingway's characters, John Grady will pass these tests with more grace than common sense. Whenever Rawlins suggests retreat, John Grady's willingness to believe in dreams forces the issue by direct confrontation. Despite the foolishness of defending Blevins, John Grady pursues the romantic dream instead of following safe advice.

In *The Crossing*'s narrative of the wolf, Billy also forces the dream of heroic possibilities. In his efforts to trap the wolf, he strives to achieve the heroic assignment given to him by his father. He uses all the ingenuity of bygone trappers and some of his own in trying to think like a wolf, to understand the very nature of it. Like Ike McCaslin, he forms a relationship with an animal's wild nature and begins to doubt his heritage. After capturing it, he faces the dilemma squarely. If he merely kills the wolf and takes it home as a bounty, he will repeat the sin of extermination and be no better than the other settlers. He will accept the pioneer's practical but limited view of the wolf as a pest, another hindrance in the western conquest of wilderness. Without allowing us to see into Billy's mind, the narrator simply tells us that "he sat the horse for a long time" (53). After apparently deciding to ride away from the dilemma, he turns back: "The wolf was watching him as before. He sat the horse a long time. The sun warm on his back. The world waiting" (53). The short sentences understate the extremity of the moment. The boy's whole future is compressed into this immediate action, and once he makes his decision, whichever way, the moment will forever split into what is and what could have been. On a whim, Billy repudiates his heritage and chooses to become a primitive-pastoral Adamic hero. For him, paradise is the dream of returning the wolf to the high Pilares. He will protect nature from encroachment and, in so doing, deny the progress of his own pioneering heritage.

The first person he meets asks him, "Have you always been crazy?" Billy's answer marks his innocence as well as his first step toward manhood: "I don't know. I never was much put to the test before today" (59). The return of the wolf is an act of redemption for the sins of mankind, for the eradication of wolves everywhere, and for turning wilderness into ranches. During the first night in the mountains, Billy looks into the wolf's eyes reflected in the campfire:

> When the flames came up her eyes burned out there like gatelamps to another world. A world burning on the shore of an unknowable void. A world construed out of blood and blood's alcahest and blood in its core and in its integument because it was that nothing save blood had power to resonate against that void which threatened hourly to devour it. He wrapped himself in the blanket and watched her. When those eyes and the nation to which they stood witness were gone at last with their dignity back into their origins there

would perhaps be other fires and other witnesses and other worlds otherwise beheld. But they would not be this one. (73–74)

These are the phrases—so prevalent in *Blood Meridian*—that remind us of the transience of all life, both animal and human. The power of the blood signifies primitive rituals that appeased the gods and covered early man's guilt for killing in the hunt and in the raid. Barbara Ehrenreich's recent study of primitive worship, *Blood Rites,* suggests that many of the sacrificial aspects of religion are part of the ancient fear of nighttime predators. The ancient sacrifices of animals and even humans to the fierce gods of night literally gave predators something to eat and would thus ensure the safety of the tribe. McCarthy here tells us that the primitive world of our ancestors is now forever unreachable by those who have long since lost the instincts to participate fully in the primacy of that world. Imaginative attempts to restore the Wild Man myth to civilized experience will never bring back the real wild men who have ceased to exist. Only in the most atavistic of men—the insane, the warriors, the primitive Adamic heroes—do we find remnants of deeper primal impulses, an animal-like affinity with the old world of tooth and claw. With the closing of the frontier, there are no wild places left for such men or such wolves. In the mountains of Old Mexico, however, Billy is searching for an Edenic sanctuary, a wilderness enclave where the wolf can live.

The American Adam persona, as a prototypical hero, is expected to demonstrate bravery and skill under duress. For the western cowboy-Adam, gunplay and horsemanship are the two standards by which he is judged. John Grady and Rawlins prove their heroic mettle in their skirmish with the Mexicans, which occurs after Blevins steals back his magnificent horse. Riding out of town under gunfire, they quickly lose their pursuers. Later in the day Rawlins makes his own deadcenter shot by killing a spikehorn buck bounding out of the juniper bush. After escaping over the mountains, John Grady and Rawlins chance upon the Eden they have been seeking:

> The grasslands lay in a deep violet haze and to the west thin flights of waterfowl were moving north before the sunset in the deep red galleries under the cloudbanks like schoolfish in a burning sea and

on the foreland plain they saw vaqueros driving cattle before them though a gauze of golden dust. (93)

The wilderness of Old Mexico gives way to a pristine garden, blooming with all the fullness of a cowboy's dream: cattle, horses, and plenty of grass. After being hired on at a hacienda, the two boys establish a local reputation by breaking a remuda of sixteen wild horses in four days, an act of western horsemanship that impresses even the old *caballeros*.

Because of his skill at roping and horsebreaking, John Grady is invited up to the ranch house, where the *hacendado*, Don Héctor, offers to share his dream of breeding mares with the great stallion. But the confidence between the two men is tainted from the start by a lie. Although Don Héctor already knows the boys are running from the incident up north, he gives John Grady a chance to explain by asking a simple question, "Why are you here?" Rather than own up to the responsibility of Blevins and the stolen horse and face the possible consequence of losing their refuge, John Grady chooses not to reveal the full truth by answering obliquely, "I just wanted to see the country, I reckon. Or we did" (113–14). The "we," of course, is only partial since Blevins is not mentioned. Gauging his response for what it is, Don Héctor continues, "May I ask how old are you?" John Grady's quick and honest answer is, "Sixteen" (114). This brings a smile from Don Héctor, when he admits that he himself had always lied about his own age when he was sixteen. So their relationship is cemented on one small truth and one enormous half-truth, which is always a half-lie. But Don Héctor does not hold the lie against John Grady. He is forgiven the larger indiscretion because of his value to the ranch and his quick honesty about his age.

As John Grady works with the great stallion, he remains mostly separated from Rawlins, his voice of reason. John Grady is soon dreaming of more than horses, as he has fallen hopelessly in love, and at first sight, with Don Héctor's daughter, Alejandra. Although he has become Don Héctor's right-hand man in all matters concerning horses, he cannot be content with this paradise without Eve. Unfortunately, the Eden John Grady has been given is a working cowboy's paradise only and does not include marriage to the daughter of a wealthy, aristocratic Mexican family.

In the first section of *The Crossing*, Billy's skills as a cowboy hero are also tested and his mettle is revealed. Like Blevins and Rawlins, Billy demonstrates considerable skill in the conventional western test of marksmanship: "In the evening a rabbit appeared in the middle of the trail a hundred feet in front of him and he reined the horse up and put two fingers to his teeth and whistled and the rabbit froze and he stepped down and shucked the rifle backward out of the scabbard and chocked it all in a single movement and raised the rifle and fired" (76). This shot hits dead center, demonstrating the worthiness of this storybook hero as a member of the hunter clan. Billy's romantic dream of returning the she-wolf to its mountain home parallels John Grady's love for Alejandra. The wolf becomes his wilderness lover as they share food and sit side by side. He drinks deeply from her eyes, soothes her like a lover, tells her stories, and sings to her (73, 74, 89). His dream for the wolf makes him appear crazy and potentially hostile to those he encounters. With wolf in tow, he disrupts the society of the trail. At one point a band of pilgrims are sent careening in all directions as the scent of the wolf sends the pack-mules bucking, strewing "baled pelts and hides and blankets and chattelgoods" down the mountain (84). In seeking his own romantic dream of nature, Billy unwittingly intrudes upon the conventions of others. A stranger in a strange land, he tramples across foreign territory without considering the possible consequences. Americans are immediately suspect in Mexico anyway, as history has demonstrated that Americans on foreign soil are usually there acting from self-interest with little regard for local customs.

John Grady soon discovers how unwelcome Americans can be in Mexico. Although he appears to be at the height of his power and influence at the hacienda, he soon pays the wages of sin. For a brief time, he lives a privileged life in a beautiful place, walking with Don Héctor, like Adam with God in the cool of the evening, as they talk about the innermost secrets of horses. This is the simple Eden he has been given, but from the beginning it is compromised. John Grady falls in love the minute he arrives, tells a lie to the figurative father-God, Don Héctor, and leaves a loose end in Blevins. In the deceptive bounty of quick success, John Grady dares to be equal with God. His love for horses like the stallion is doubled in his "ardenthearted" pursuit of Alejandra. Soon the stallion, Rawlins, his job, his respect for Don Héctor, all of what has enabled him to live at the hacienda, are a distant second to his unstoppable love: "John Grady loved to ride the horse. In truth he loved to be seen riding it. In truth he loved for her to see him riding it" (127). The earlier half-lie has led to the lie of having to ride the stallion, which grows into the lie of letting Alejandra ride the stallion, which grows into a complete betrayal of Don Héctor's trust.

In his fevered state, John Grady cannot see anything beyond the all-encompassing present of his beautiful dream girl. She appears "in that wild summer landscape: real horse, real rider, real land and sky and yet a dream withal" (132). The reality of his position and of hers is completely obscured by the pressure of his storybook dream, despite a very pointed warning from Dueña Alfonsa to consider the girl's reputation. Another indirect warning is delivered by Rawlins, who reminds him that "the spread" is attached to the girl and therein lies the rub. When John Grady doesn't seem to understand, Rawlins speaks the plain truth:

> I know the old man likes you, said Rawlins. But that don't mean he'll set still for you courtin his daughter.
> Yeah, I know.
> I don't see you holdin no aces.
> Yeah.
> What I see is you fixin to get us fired and run off the place. (138)

But an Adam is never moved by the mundane truth of tomorrow's severe consequences or threats from above. Like the biblical Adam who chooses Eve over God, John Grady cannot see beyond the moment, "sweeter for the larceny of time and flesh, sweeter for the betrayal" (141). Once his dream ground is staked out, there is no retreat. It is akin to the *querencia* of the bullring, the defensive, territorial holding of one's own turf. Like the bull, the machismo of unshakable resolve represents the ideal of American manhood. Adam's imaginative capacity to dream in itself becomes a sin of pride and appears nothing but foolish, or crazy, to more levelheaded bystanders.

The progress myth of the American Adam is standard fare in westerns. Critic Will Wright delineates the conventional "classic plot" in terms that accurately describe the action of *All the Pretty Horses* thus far. The cowboy hero, cut off from his roots, restless and nomadic, comes in unknown from the wilderness and enters a well-defined social group. Through tests of manhood, he demonstrates exceptional ability and as a result is given special status. The most beautiful female of the group takes a romantic interest and love blossoms, but the society does not fully trust or accept the hero because of his mysterious past (Wright 48). *All the Pretty Horses* transcends the formulaic western in its beautiful prose and literary technique; underneath, McCarthy is retelling the same classic myth.

One primary difference between the primitive-pastoral and the progress myth is the latter's use of stock villains. In the primitive-pastoral, the enemy is the abstract force of progress, often embodied in evil corporations or governments representing the encroaching, malevolent authority of oppressive society. In the progress myth, which promotes Anglo-American interests, the villains are concrete and nonwhite. In the silent-movie era, the mustachioed bandit with his crossed bandolier of bullets reflected prevailing American views of Pancho Villa and other bandits from the Mexican Revolution. Despite a brief period during World War I when the "Hun" replaced the Mexican villain, "greaser" as a racial slur came back into widespread prominence during the twenties and thirties. By the forties, two cultural forces virtually ended this ethnic stereotype for nearly two decades. Federal administrations, fearing infiltration from Germany and Japan into Mexico, pressed the Good Neighbor policy onto the media at the same time that Mexico and other Latin American countries were vigorously protesting and boycotting studios whose films contained racist Latin stereotypes. In the forties and fifties, Mexicans were generally not portrayed as bandidos since the Germans, Japanese, and Russians filled the national requirement for villains. The bandido villain was revived in the sixties, most notably in Sergio Leone's spaghetti westerns and Sam Peckinpah's western films (Slatta, *Bandidos* 36–59).

The evil bandido image is introduced in *All the Pretty Horses* in the form of the Mexican captain. He immediately strips the boys and demands to know why they have come to Mexico and whether Blevins is their brother. Since Blevins has already killed a man while trying to retrieve his horse, the captain has very little patience, repeatedly referring to him as the "assassin Blevins." Suddenly, John Grady's willful dreams of working with the stallion and seeing Alejandra are shattered and replaced by a descent into the purgatory of prison.

Likewise, in *The Crossing,* the foreign other of Mexican society unexpectedly stops Billy from achieving his primitive-pastoral dream. With his destination in sight, the "high wild ranges of the Pilares Teras," Billy is arrested for having no papers (93–95). The wolf is confiscated and sent to a local fair. Although Billy has been operating illegally on his own romantic whim, he is released to go home. Instead of accepting defeat and returning to his ranch a fool, Billy steels himself and resolves to continue. He will not be foiled by Mexican society and, as a result, soon finds himself in conflict with the local customs. Among the people, great tales are told of how the wolf was caught after eating many schoolchildren, or how it was captured with a wild boy who ran naked through the woods, or how werewolves followed the hunting party, howling at night. At the dogfights, the *hacendado* relates how he has heard that the American was caught stealing the wolf from the Pilares Teras and had been "intent on taking the wolf to his own country where he would sell the animal at some price" (118). Here McCarthy portrays the chameleonlike ability of myths to transmute into whatever form is most desired by a particular audience. Later, in the novel's second subplot—after Boyd accidentally kills the *manco—campesinos* from the area likewise form a myth of their own and celebrate it in a *corrido*. In the mythic version, Boyd becomes a daring, brave defender of the lower classes by striking a blow against the corrupt manco, "who had not reckoned upon the great heart of the güerito" (318). As McCarthy demonstrates, the truth of what really happened is quickly lost, and popular myth far surpasses it.

But just as John Grady is unwilling to curtail his dream of seeing Alejandra or retrieving Blevins's horse, so is Billy unable to walk away from the wolf. Despite having had pistols drawn against him once already, he returns to the dogfights. The hacendado has clearly warned him with plain speech, even using English:

You think that this country is some country you can come here and do what you like.
I never thought that. I never thought about this country one way

or the other.

Yes, said the hacendado.

We was just passin through, the boy said. We wasn't bothering nobody. Queríamos pasar, no más. (119)

Billy's belligerent response reveals a pastoral hero's defiance of authority. Parents and society negate youthful dreams, intrude on passionate idealism. Billy is not only oblivious but scornful of cultural differences and protocol. The hacendado's authority is no better than his father's, for it has overruled his own pastoral vision of truth. In a moment of pure existential action, a sort of primal scream of being, Billy goes back to reclaim his vision. He boldly enters the arena and fires his rifle into the head of his beloved wolf, putting a stop to the animal's ordeal. One way or another, Billy will end what he has begun. His life has been on a trajectory toward this moment since that first lingering moment of turning back to observe the trapped wolf. Although his pastoral dream of a primitive wilderness paradise is shattered, he still does not yield to authority; he remains true to himself and faithful to a hero's code of honor, whatever the cost. Once a dream is formed, a hero brings it to fruition, regardless of danger.

In *All the Pretty Horses,* John Grady and Rawlins pay the personal cost for bringing social upheaval to their cowboy paradise when John Grady and Alejandra become lovers. Adam's mother-protector, Dueña Alfonsa, cannot save him now from the wrath of the garden's father-God, Don Héctor. So John Grady is cast out of the garden he would dare to rule; he cannot be equal with God. Society always deals with antiheroes who subvert codified wisdom, who trample old conventions for nothing more than the ardor of youth. After the boys' arrest, the lost dream of cowboy paradise revisits John Grady one last time in his sleep:

That night he dreamt of horses in a field on a high plain where the spring rains had brought up the grass and the wildflowers out of the ground and the flowers ran all blue and yellow far as the eye could see and in the dream he was among the horses running and in the dream he himself could run with the horses and they coursed the young mares and fillies over the plain where their rich bay and their rich chestnut colors shone in the sun and the young colts ran with their dams and trampled down the flowers in a haze of pollen that hung in the sun like powdered gold.... (161)

John Grady, Rawlins, and Blevins are abruptly thrown into the harsh world—the "thorns and tares"—of prison, which Gail Morrison calls "Blakean in its divisions and also reminiscent of Melville in the malevolent and omnipotent presence of evil" (180). The demigod of this hell is the self-appointed captain, who speaks bluntly to John Grady about the nature of truth and reality: "You see. We can make the truth here. Or we can lose it. But when you leave here it will be too late. Too late for truth. Then you will be in the hands of other parties. Who can say what the truth will be then? At that time?" (168). Like Billy, John Grady refuses to acknowledge authority, and he takes Blevins's side despite the danger, because he still feels somehow responsible for this younger double of himself. They have both ridden into Mexico like some kind of Rough Riders, blithely expecting that they have a natural right to exist and can devise rules of their own choosing without regard for Mexican law.

Not even the harsh reality of a Mexican prison breaks John Grady's stubborn independence or his idealistic confidence in his own best judgment. He remains defiant to the evil captain during interrogations, while Rawlins becomes readily malleable under the new circumstances. In the midnight scene at the prison in Saltillo, after Blevins's execution, John Grady doesn't listen as the captain tries to tell them the basics of survival in the prison environment:

> You are not the first Americans to be here, said the captain. In this place. I have friends in this place and you will be making these arrangements with these peoples. I don't want you to make no mistakes.
> We don't have any money, said John Grady. We aint fixin to make any arrangements.
> Excuse me but you will be making some arrangements. You don't know nothing.
> What did you do with our horses.
> We are not talking about horses now. Those horses must wait. The

rightful owners must be found of those horses.

Rawlins stared bleakly at John Grady. Just shut the hell up, he said. (180)

As the pragmatic one, Rawlins understands the obvious common sense of not inciting trouble. John Grady, however, shares Blevins's inability to see his limits and thus does not know where his authority ends and the world's begins. For idealists, radicals, extremists, to be young and "ardenthearted" is everything, and any limits to their own will seem insubstantial, mere gossamer hindrances to be brushed aside.

Surprisingly, the captain identifies with, even sees himself in, John Grady's refusal to acknowledge other people's reality and to insist on making up his own rules. He tells the boys, "I am the one when I go someplace then there is no laughing. When I go there then they stop laughing" (181). His early discomfort in being laughed at as a child leads to the discovery that he can dominate others. As a victim himself, the captain has learned the power of control. This truth is the evil double of the romantic's truth. Both a hero and a villain believe their own particular position in the world is superior and that they can triumph by sheer willpower. And both will break the rules to achieve their own ends. The difference between the two types is purely one of motives. The hero acts according to the ideals of love and beauty, while the villain seeks self-gratification in the perverse sadistic need to dominate. The main conflict of any mythic story revolves around the twinned opposed wills to control and dominate others. As an American Adam, John Grady does not relent when warned about romancing Alejandra, and he does not relent in prison when warned by the captain.

In *The Crossing,* Billy's determination to return the wolf's carcass to the mountains does not fulfill the promise of his original dream. Instead, he embarks on a pilgrimage of self-abasement (130), seeking redemption in a mountain purgatory. In a symbolic act of contrition, he seeks redemption for all settlers who ever trapped wolves, despoiling the pristine garden. Billy's original assignment from his father—a voice of authority and reason—would have led to other domestic responsibilities and a conventional sort of manhood. Trapping and killing the wolf would have demonstrated his mastery as a hunter-rancher within the progress mythos.

He would have continued the work of subduing the land, taming the West. Without that first willful, loving act of turning back to observe the wolf, to see into its soul, Billy would not have been launched into the role of a primitive-pastoral hero. Because he does turn, in the instant of becoming one with the wolf the pioneer boy is transformed into a pastoral rebel who seeks redemption for his people's transgressions. As he ascends into the mountains, he exchanges innocence for experience; his youthful idealism is broken on the hard reality of Mexican history. He crosses a point of no return; he cannot go back and become a conventional pioneer, and he cannot recreate a lost Eden. He is left with penance, an ascetic period of atonement for his people's crimes. The act of dragging the wolf carcass to its natural home also foreshadows the macabre sequence later in the novel when he retrieves Boyd's body. After the ceremony of burying the wolf, Billy lingers for weeks in the high-mountain wilderness, reverting to a Wild Man, fashioning a bow out of a holly limb and arrows from cane. He regresses to an early Neolithic state as a hunter. He shoots a hawk out of the air with the rudimentary arrows. He becomes gaunt like a supplicant monk who has taken a vow of primitivism. He undergoes a redemptive revitalization, a divine state of madness, mutilating his body in a ritual shedding of blood, cutting his hand with a knife, reenacting Christ's stigmata (130). He hallucinates and witnesses strange miracles: "Two days later he sat the horse on a promontory overlooking the Bavispe River and the river was running backwards. That or the sun was setting in the east behind him" (130). He peers into the mysteries of a dying fire, "the red crazings in the woodcoals where they broke along their unguessed gridlines. As if in the trying of the wood were elicited hidden geometries and their orders which could only stand fully revealed, such is the way of the world, in darkness and ashes. He heard no wolves" (130). He will never be able to save even one wolf, or save his brother, or in *Cities of the Plain,* to save John Grady. Throughout *The Crossing,* Billy finds no permanent peace, no final Eden, no ultimate atonement. The pastoral quest itself must suffice. The gleaming ideal of paradise beckons youth to grand ventures, but experience teaches the young that dreams are always short-lived. The best of life is found in the brief ardor of idealism. Billy comes out of the mountains with more challenges to face and more hard lessons to learn in what proves to be a cyclic pattern. The pastoral myth sequence is replayed—dreaming of paradise, near attainment of the dream, overreaching what is possible, finally loss and purgatory. Then the whole process begins again.

In part two of the novel, Billy's dream to take his brother into Mexico and retrieve their stolen horses is just as far-fetched as the dream of restoring the wolf. And as in the first part, Billy meets with disaster—losing Boyd, first to a gunshot wound and then to the love of a woman. Along the way the two boys are warned by older, wiser counsel in the form of McCarthy's anchorites, who materialize along the trail to offer gloomy, oblique advice concerning the mystery of life, how a man's will is not the stuff of reality but rather a striving of "doomed enterprises [that] divide lives forever into the then and the now" (129). But the advice is never taken, as the boys venture on, seeking their impossible dreams and rebelling against authority.

In both novels, the history of Mexico serves as an example of Eden conceived and lost. In *The Crossing,* a blind man's wife recounts the story of how her idealistic young husband sought glory in the Revolution by fighting for Herrera. Facing overwhelming odds, her husband could escape with the more practical soldiers but instead refuses to leave his post and is captured. In captivity he is generously offered amnesty if, and only if, he swears an oath of fealty to the government. But remaining true to his rebellious, idealistic vision of paradise, he refuses to save himself and is lined up to be "shot without ceremony" (276). A captain in the federal army lectures the prisoners on the pathetic foolishness of dying for "a cause that was both wrong and doomed" (276). When the young man defiantly spits in the captain's face, his eyes are sucked from their sockets and left hanging to slowly dry. (McCarthy's use of the grotesque image here is reminiscent of *Blood Meridian*'s graphic violence.) With the loss of his eyesight, the young man's idealism shrivels as well.[2]

In another example of Mexico's failed dreams, Dueña Alfonsa gives John Grady her personal account of the tragic history of the Revolution: "In the Spaniard's heart is a great yearning for freedom, but only his own. A great love of truth and honor in all its forms, but not in its substance. And a deep conviction that nothing can be proven except that it be made to bleed. Virgins, bulls, men. Ultimately God himself" (*All the Pretty Horses* 231). Despite the idealism of the people, the Revolution degenerates into another example of Girard's contagion of mindless violence. Dueña Alfonsa warns John Grady, "What is constant in history is greed and foolishness and a love of blood" (239); against the ideal of Mexican democracy is the reality that in 1911 Francisco Madero "became the first president of this republic ever to be placed in office by popular vote. And the last" (236). Those who died in the Revolution become empty sacrifices, meaningless to any real social progress, part of the larger failed dream of the whole Revolution. Like so many of McCarthy's characters, Alfonsa ponders the relationships between free will, chance, and fate: "The question for me was always whether that shape we see in our lives was there from the beginning or whether these random events are only called a pattern after the fact. Because otherwise we are nothing" (230). And like so many of McCarthy's older characters, she is unable to untangle enough of the puppet strings of life to trace in them any definite meaning. Although Alfonsa was once a young idealist herself, as an old woman she becomes entrenched in the intractable society she once detested. Throughout the Border Trilogy, young heroes always reject such older voices of wisdom, stubbornly defying chance and fate and the authority of society in favor of their own indomitable will.

McCarthy's protagonists heroically stand firm, maintaining defiant idealism in the face of death. It is a part of the ancient warrior's code of honor to fight with tenacious nobility and determined grace while remaining true to his cause. It is Hegel's concept of "the bloody battle," which assigns a "moral weight" to pride and the willingness to risk one's life (Fukuyama 155). The Adamic hero of the American West is an adaptation of the ancient male code of honor, found among most warrior cultures. Norman Mailer was the first writer to label the transplanted code of the New World Garden "American existentialism," noting that a typical hero (a black man, in his example) defies the authority of society and excels in "the enormous present" and the "art of the primitive" (Noble 205). Our American mythic code in its primitive-pastoral version differs from the old European code of chivalry in that loyalty is never pledged to an imperial authority but instead to the passionate exigencies of the self and pastoral dreams. What makes our Adam "existential" becomes clear when he sees an opportunity to reach for the forbidden fruit: even when he fails, the American Adam holds fast to his original desire, refusing to relent or submit. The forces arrayed against him are like a fire that tempers the steel of his will, forging it into a weapon. A defiant Adam prefers to fight for the freedom of the wilderness rather than to abide by the rules of Eden.

After almost dying in a bloody knife fight, John Grady attempts, once more, to achieve his dream of marrying Alejandra. He soon discovers, however, that in his brave new post-Edenic world, Alejandra has sacrificed her love for him as a down payment on his release from prison, arranged by his mother-protector, Dueña Alfonsa. As his benefactress, she sees a parallel between her own youthful idealism in Alejandra's situation, but as a surrogate mother and member of aristocratic society, she knows John Grady is unfit to fill the position to which he aspires. In effect, she agrees with Don Héctor's decision to expel John Grady from the hacienda. Although he meets Alejandra once more, he fails to entice her with a far-fetched dream of eloping together and escaping from society altogether. Alejandra plainly tells him that she still suffers from the loss of her father's love and yearns to reestablish her former position in the family more than she desires John Grady. While walking with him one last time, she points to the place where her grandfather died in the Revolution and talks about how all romantic dreams end in Mexico, comparing "the Street of Desire" to the "Calle de Noche Triste" (Street of Sad Night) (*All the Pretty Horses* 253). In effect, Alejandra trades love for history and becomes another Dueña Alfonsa as she abandons her romantic, defiant posture for one of meek compliance.

John Grady's idealistic desire for success in a desperate venture quickly transfers from Alejandra back to the storybook horses. In another sequence of defiant existential action, he kidnaps the evil captain—partly to assuage his disappointment in love and partly in revenge for Blevins's death, but more important to finish what he had once begun. As a hero in the classic progress myth, John Grady will retrieve American property. He is now acting in the best interests of Anglo-Americans, opposing the evil Mexican villain by boldly invading his turf. In the sequence where he takes the captain hostage, recaptures the horses, and evades the posse, we see the classic "good" American defeating the foreign enemy. The captain's defeat reassures a traditional Anglo audience that ugly, evil men in foreign lands are still made accountable for their crimes against American interests.

When John Grady leaves the weakened, sniveling captain to his fate at the hands of the mountain people, readers feel that the world is a better place. In the courtroom scene at the end of this subplot, John Grady is granted a representative Anglo-American audience who readily appreciates the heroics of the boy's action against the Mexican captain. The judge not only finds him innocent of any wrongdoing but commends him for bravery. His amazing testimony of using a hot pistol barrel to cauterize his own wounds causes "absolute silence in the courtroom" (289). The boy has returned a man and has the war wounds to prove it. The judge, with typical western reserve, says, "I've heard a lot of things that give me grave doubts about the human race but this aint one of em" (289). Later that night in a less formal visit with the judge, John Grady again tries to sort out the moral ambiguities of his foray into Mexico, but the judge assures him that he has not acted immorally, because he has acted from the heart, thus justifying the violent ramifications of his behavior. Although he offers no real solace for the killing, which he admits is always difficult even when men are evil, his final advice to the kid is simply to get on with life. The judge represents closure in the classic plot of western progress by approving of John Grady's defeat of the foreign Other.

Mark Busby believes that the act of participating in killing represents the primary challenge for the American Adam. Death, whether of opponents or allies, shakes the hero's illusion of peace and forces him to face the extreme consequences of his own rebellion: "Usually the main character must face the reality of death; either his own life is threatened or he witnesses the death of another character. The resulting awareness dawns slowly in most cases, suggesting a gap between seeing and understanding and the difficulty in overcoming illusions" (100). The redemption of the Adamic hero can never be found by accepting authority or following conventional advice but instead must come from within the hero's own being. He must reconcile what he has seen and done with his own conscience and struggle to incorporate the experience within his mythic code of dreaming big and winning at any cost.

When John Grady visits the real Jimmy Blevins, a radio evangelist, in search of answers to his vague yearning for closure, it gives him comfort, as if he has made a surrogate visit to Blevins's parents even though they are no relation to the strange kid who had assumed their name. After dinner, Blevins's wife comically reaffirms the novel's theme by proudly recounting the triumphs of her idealistic husband, noting that his voice can be heard all over the world and even on Mars: "And Jimmy Blevins done it. He was the one" (*All the Pretty Horses* 298). One man's will retains the power to reach out and heroically transform reality into the shape of his own dreams.

The Crossing's last heroic sequence also reaffirms man's capacity to dream and fail and live to dream again in a mythic cycle. After Billy fails in many attempts to get himself enlisted in the army, he sets off on another journey to Mexico, this time to bring his brother home. In a sequence reminiscent of Cal's stubborn determination to fulfill a similar promise to Gus in Larry McMurtry's *Lonesome Dove,* Billy hauls the bones of his brother all the way back, encountering danger from bandits and flooded rivers. As in the strange parallel scene (another of McCarthy's doublings) in which the "bones" of an airplane are being laboriously hauled out of the mountains by gypsies, Billy is likewise set on a dream which proves to be "most difficult" (*The Crossing* 406).

By the final scenes of the two novels, the boy protagonists have grown into men, but neither character will find happiness. The shared fate of both kinds of mythic Adam, progressive and primitive-pastoral, is to be banished from the comforts of domesticity. Although they have passed the traditional western tests of manhood and have been seasoned by experiences in the wilderness, they remain drifters, defiant and alone, unyielding in their determination to see their dreams fulfilled. After witnessing defeat and the deaths of friends and relatives, they retain the spark of idealism and move on to the next dream. As Andrew Ettin notes, the certain knowledge of death reinforces their idealism: "Death, the great leveler, makes us all pastoral characters, and therefore the knowledge that death must come should make our earthly pastoral world that much more precious to us. . . . Against the marmoreal chill of death, life on this bountiful earth, filled with moments of small yet important pleasures, is itself pastoral" (qtd. in Love 201). The fate of McCarthy's protagonists, like that of all mythic cowboys, is to remain restless, roaming, and sublimely lonely. Billy's unanswered call to the old, mangy dog is the call for his long-dead she-wolf and for Boyd, that he might complete what he has started (Hall, "Hero as Philosopher" 194): "He took off his hat and placed it on the tarmac before him and he bowed his head and held his face in his hands and wept. He sat there for a long time and after a while the east did gray and after a while the right and godmade sun did rise, once again, for all and without distinction" (*The Crossing* 426). The denouement of this narrative does not allow for any kind of easy resolution, since the American Adam continually replays the mythic cycle of regeneration and loss. His discoveries are found inside himself instead of in the resolution of decisive action. As a romantic hero, the American Adam repeatedly throws himself against the hard truths of authority. This struggle ennobles his character and creates existential moments of heroic defiance—often full of that elusive Hemingway quality known as "grace under pressure."

Five

Thematic Motifs in *Cities of the Plain*

"Our plans are predicated upon a future unknown to us."
—from *Cities of the Plain*

Who's afraid of the dark? We all are, or should be. Compared to other animals with more developed senses of hearing and smell, as well as enhanced night vision, we are limited by our inability to see clearly in the dark. Being afraid of the dark is as primal as fear gets. We have been cowering around campfires since the first evening of mankind—and not just to stay warm. There might be dangers lurking out there beyond the perimeter of our light: big cats, bears, wolves, crocodiles, snakes. Ancient common sense, a sixth sense, warns us to be wary of the night. Seeing has always been our best way of discerning what is actual. To see is to believe; blindness is fear. But to the most daring and romantic of us—poets, cowboys, and lunatics—night is more like a different shade of day, a place to muse and ride and dream. Some of us are blind to the dangers of night because we cannot see the darkness.

For McCarthy's cowboys, the night bodes ill. In the dark, Billy flicks the switch on the barn lights and is jolted by the current running through faulty wiring. Shaking his arm in pain, he recalls past misadventures: "Ever time I reach for that son of a bitch I get shocked" (13). The larger "son of a bitch" in this novel is Mexico, and the faulty switch presages a return to the theme of romantic tragedy across the border. Mexico at night is wholly alien to a cowboy's daytime existence. In the stark light of day, ranching is simple, straightforward, and rewarding. As Billy aptly puts it, a cowboy's work ethic is to "put in a day's work for a day's wages. . . . Daybreak to backbreak for a godgiven dollar" (10). And Billy, like any Adamic hero living in a cowboy's Eden, understands the life-sustaining, redemptive rewards of an honest day's work. In a burst of exuberance he gushes, "I love this life. You love this life, son? I love this life. You do love this life don't you? Cause by god I love it. Just love it" (10). Billy affirms the value of Mac's ranch and of having a stable position. The wanderlust of the first two novels is absent here; after all their journeys, John Grady and Billy have finally found a home. For readers familiar with the other novels in the Border Trilogy, Billy's top-of-the-morning exuberance for ranch life recalls the lost paradises of the pair's childhood family ranches and of Don Héctor's hacienda. In *Cities of the Plain,* McCarthy raises the stakes to tragic proportions. He locates his two cowboy heroes several years after the close of *All the Pretty Horses* in a ranch paradise outside El Paso, replete with all the familiar trimmings: cows, horses, dogs, and all the biscuits and gravy and scrambled eggs and grits and sausage and preserves and *pico de gallo* and butter and honey his men can eat. There is much to lose here.

From the beginning, McCarthy laces the text with motifs from one of his favorite themes: man's inability to predict far-reaching consequences of his actions. Upon a first reading of the novel, most of the oblique motifs are fleeting, such as the moment that follows Billy's expression of love for a cowboy's life: "The sun was blinding white on the dusty windshield glass" (10). Only later does one realize that this detail is part of a repeating pattern of blindness from reflections. Shortly thereafter, a coyote trots along the crest of a nearby ridge, paying no attention to the men. Billy notices the coyote first: "I want you to look at that son of a bitch" (11). The phrasing connects this scene with the faulty light switch, which is also a "son of a bitch" (13). John Grady underestimates the coyote's abilities when he suggests going for his rifle and taking a shot. Billy informs him that the coyote would "be gone before you get done standin up" (11). Unsettled by such an unnatural sight in "the middle of the day," John Grady wonders, "You think he seen us?" and Billy answers with typical western aplomb, "I don't expect he was completely blind" (12). John Grady's surprise and desire to reach for a gun underscore his misunderstanding of night creatures as well as his preference for direct action. In contrast, Billy establishes himself as the older voice of experience and restraint.

Small, unsettling moments resonate in the episode leading up to the incident when an owl crashes into the ranch truck. Late at night, on the road back to the ranch, Billy drives past a stranded truckload of Mexicans in need of help. After continuing on without stopping, he abruptly changes his mind and turns back, remembering a time eleven years before, after Boyd had been shot, when he and his brother were helped by such people. The brothers were rescued from the "worst day of my life," as he explains to Troy: "We was on the run and he was hurt and there was a truckload of Mexicans just about like them back yonder appeared out of nowhere and pulled our bacon out of the fire" (36). In playing the good "Samaritan," as Troy puts it, Billy pays some interest on a past debt. However, Troy, who does not trust Mexicans as a general rule, suspects that the travelers may be lying about heading for Sanderson and suggests that nothing Mexican should be taken at face value. Although this blatant comment surprises Billy—who replies "Why would anybody lie about goin to Sanderson Texas?" (34)—its truth is later borne out by the novel's denouement, which, as in *All the Pretty Horses* and *The Crossing,* involves an existential hero who defies authority. Against all odds and sensible advice, John Grady persists in acting according to his own will. He will sacrifice all for love. Unforeseen troubles presage John Grady's eventual martyrdom. When Billy turns back to help the Mexicans fix a flat tire, he inadvertently sets in motion events leading to the accident with the owl.

Billy and John Grady share an affinity for Mexican folk *campesinos* and a faith in their country hospitality. Like cowboys, campesinos live close to the land and are poor, hardworking, and honest. They also live according to a machismo code of honor and suffer at the hands of authority. Likewise, campesino culture endows young rebels with legendary status. The songs of the Border, known as *corridos,* celebrate the exploits of cowboys who willingly pit themselves against corrupt landowners or Anglos.[1] Fighting oppression, these antiheroes sacrifice themselves in a hail of bullets as martyrs to the people's causes. Travis speaks for cowboys in general as he fondly recalls frequent trips into Old Mexico:

> Mostly I just visited. I liked it. I liked the country and I liked the people in it. I rode all over Chihuahua and a good part of Coahuila and some of Sonora. I'd be gone weeks at a time and not have hardly so much as a peso in my pocket but it didnt make no difference. Those people would take you in and put you up and feed you and feed your horse and cry when you left. You could of stayed forever. They didn't have nothin. Never had and never would. But you could stop at some little estancia in the absolute dead center of nowhere and they'd take you in like you was kin. (90)

While John Grady looks out over the beautiful landscape, "the green line of the river breaks and range on range [of] distant mountains," he muses nostalgically about his own adventures in Mexico, telling Billy, "Those people would take you in. Hide you out. Lie for you. No one ever asked me what it was I'd done" (217). Although both men retain a love for campesino culture, in *Cities of the Plain* Billy has outgrown his youthful, naïve attraction to Mexico's romantic possibilities. At twenty-eight, he is nine years older than John Grady, more travel-worn and world-weary. In contrast with John Grady's youthful optimism, the tone of Billy's reply reveals bitterness over the loss of the wolf and his brother Boyd: "I went down there three separate trips. I never once come back with what I started after" (217). Billy is more wary of life's vicissitudes and no longer yearns for adventure or love. He has become practical over the years, settling into the comforts of electric light and stable ranch life. His character in this novel is a dramatic change from the young existential hero who rescued a wolf in *The Crossing*, as he now joins the ranks of reason and caution, much like Rawlins in *All the Pretty Horses*. Billy is old for his twenty-eight years, and has learned "hard lessons in this world," like Mr. Johnson, who tells John Grady the hardest lesson in life is "that when things are gone they're gone. They aint comin' back" (126), citing the extinction of wolves in the Southwest as an example. Of course, in *The Crossing*, a much younger Billy has learned firsthand the impossibility of saving even one wolf. In his new role as pragmatic older brother, Billy advises John Grady to give up his impossible, romantic dreams, to stop playing the fool, to see things as they really are, not as he wishes them to be. Billy himself has ignored such advice several times as a young man, as has John Grady in *All the Pretty Horses*. Throughout the Border Trilogy, the existential, Adamic hero never takes the path of least resistance. Instead, he behaves according to the unyielding ethics required in the cowboy's code of honor, in which a man is expected to act spontaneously from the heart while stubbornly ignoring all-too-certain ramifications of the deed.

Billy will not leave a truckload of campesinos stranded. Instead, he turns around and helps the Mexicans repair the flat. On this night, at least, he will act heroically, like John Grady, and not worry about the unforeseeable consequences of kindness. He owes a debt to the Mexicans for helping his brother Boyd. McCarthy gives us a visual clue to this incident's connection with the Mexican prostitute Magdalena in the description of the Mexicans' truck, which has a faulty taillight with a short in it, and thus winks "on and off like a signal" (33). The faulty wiring of the taillight is doubled in the wiring of the barn light, which shocks Billy when he flips the switch (13). It also finds a resonance later in a Juárez café scene, where a "man with a strange device" asks John Grady if he wishes "to electrocute himself" (37). The motif of winking reappears in the winking eye of Magdalena's ominous servant and the sudden appearance of Eduardo's knife in the climactic fight. By connecting "the old one-eyed criada" (72), whose blinking eye makes her appear "to be winking in some suggestive complicity" (101) to "a wink of light off the blade" (247), McCarthy's overlapping images make the symbolism clear: the night of Mexico is full of winking hazards, and stopping to act the part of Good Samaritan entails fatal consequences.

Soon after Billy stops to help the Mexicans, an owl slams into the truck, breaking the windshield, "a sudden white flare" (34) recalling the earlier sun "blinding white on the dusty windshield glass" (10). The "laminate of the glass" is "belled in softly." In death, the owl sprawls "cruciform" across the "wrecked glass" like an "enormous moth in a web" (34). With symbolism suggesting a Christlike crucifixion, the "soft and downy" bird, "its head slumped and rolled," is hung by the men on the wires of a nearby fence (34). The owl incident also foreshadows John Grady's nighttime plunge into the fatal knife fight with Eduardo. The fractured windshield of Billy's truck prefigures John Grady kicking in the doorglass of Eduardo's car, which is described in similar terms: "The glass was laminated and it spidered whitely in the light and sagged inward" (246). John Grady replays the role of the crucified owl, which is normally at home in the night until it is unexpectedly blindsided by a car. Finally, shortly before their last night together, John Grady and Magdalena may be seen in the description of two owls: "Two owls crouching in the dust of the road turned their pale and heartshaped faces in the trucklights and blinked and rose on their white wings as silent as two souls ascending and vanished in the darkness overhead" (201).

The small pathos of the owl accident is one of many such unnatural occurrences involving blindness followed by the sudden tragic clarity of death. Blindness can be interpreted as both the literal condition of inability to see and the figurative condition of being unable to foretell the future. Both omens are bad. The identity of the owl, whose death disturbs Billy and Troy, is richly connotative, suggesting Billy's dead brother, Boyd; Troy's dead brother, John; and the future death of John Grady. Blindness in foreseeing the consequences of doomed love raises the mythic stakes to tragic proportions. A pastoral hero loves unwisely, which inevitably leads to an existential moment, a choice between paternal advice and youthful passion. Pastoral poets—from Sidney and Shakespeare to Yeats and Graves—have demonstrated the pattern. True love is an unquenchable, eternal force of human nature. It is sexual and ideological, like an Adamic hero who sacrifices the safety of his father's Eden for Eve's love. And he never sees the consequences. A pastoral hero is blinded by his own willful idealism—unable to see the folly of his actions and unwilling to accept the advice of more level-headed friends.

Various characters in *Cities of the Plain* demonstrate the power of true love. Mac's love for his dead wife continues unabated, as does Mr. Johnson's love for his dead daughter. The unfulfilled promise of love can be seen in the old rancher who picks up John Grady even as he goes to fight Eduardo. When, speaking of his wife, he tells the boy, "There aint been a day passed in sixty years I aint thanked God for that woman" (235), it underscores the extent of John Grady's tragic loss: a lifetime with Magdalena that is never to be. Love's power over John Grady is such that he will not—cannot—give it up. As Troy says about Grady, "I reckon he just don't like to quit a horse" (16). As we have seen in *All the Pretty*

Horses, in John Grady's passion for Alejandra, in the cowboy's pastoral scheme of things a horse is a lot like a woman. When Billy tells Troy that he once lost a horse he "was awful partial to," Troy's double-entendre rejoinder, "It's easy to do," applies to women as well (23). Horses and women inspire cowboys to existential acts of true love.

Blindness from reflections at night proves fatal. As Billy and Troy drive back to the ranch, a jackrabbit freezes in the road and is hit (20). This leads to Troy's tall tale about killing a hundred jackrabbits on a wild road trip. Figuratively, the jackrabbits represent John Grady's blindness to reality. Recalling his night rides with Don Héctor's stallion, John Grady says, "I used to love to ride of a night . . . You'll see things on the desert that you can't understand" (124). When he is asked what sort of things are in the night, he explains that horses can see a lot more than their riders and intimates that a horse's vision is more reliable, a vision into the deeper meaning of life itself: "I aint talkin about spooks. It's more like just the way things are. If you only knew it" (124). Like a jackrabbit, John Grady is attracted to the night and its dangerous reflections. At one point, Billy directly warns the younger man about riding at night: "Ride him blind through the brush tryin to beat me back. Get him snakebit and I don't know what all" (181). But John Grady replies with characteristic cowboy machismo, "It takes a special hand to ride him in the dark. . . . A rider that can instill confidence in a animal" (181). This kind of blind faith in his nocturnal abilities indicates John Grady's tragic flaw, hubris, which leads him to search for Magdalena in the dark, dangerous lights of Mexico. During his meeting with her, he opens his heart completely, confiding to her his past, the events described in *All the Pretty Horses.* He tells her about the old Comanche trail and "how he would ride that trail in the moonlight in the fall of the year when he was a boy" (205). Later, he tells her about his plans to rescue her from Eduardo and blithely reassures her there is nothing to fear. Despite previous lessons about the dangers of Mexico, he has not yet learned to be afraid of its dark.

One plausible explanation for the long gaps between McCarthy's novels—years in length—may be the richness of intricately associated motifs that they require. He works and reworks a novel to achieve figurative saturation, adding visual and verbal cues until every scene resonates with symbolic overlays. In *Cities of the Plain,* such thematic motifs all point in one direction: toward the final knife fight.

In the ribald humor of the novel's first pages, it is easy to overlook the small details of the setting: "Out in the street the rain slashed through the standing water driving the gaudy red and green colors of the neon signs to wander and seethe" (3). The rain violently cuts like knives through the gaudy, wet silk-shirt-like neon lights, green and bleeding with red. And just so we don't forget later on, in the "bloodred barlight" the cowboys salute "some fourth companion now lost to them" (3). Thus an intimation of John Grady's death is already present in their toast. Images of rain, red lights, and red carpet proliferate in McCarthy's descriptions of the streets and whorehouses of Juárez. As they walk up Juárez Avenue, "the lights of the bars and cafes and curioshops bled slowly in the wet black street" (7). The trolley tracks "shining in the wet lamplight" run "like great surgical clamps" toward the ominous "dark shapes of the mountains" (7). The pouring rain that floods the streets and soaks their boots at several points in the narrative parallels the loss of blood in the climactic knifefight. When John Grady returns to La Venada to look for Magdalena, a "small drip of water falling from the ceiling into puddles in the bloodred carpeting" suggests the dripping of blood from wounds (55). Later, in John Grady's dream, the velour curtains are "as red as blood" (103). And on the last night of his life, he stands and watches "the sky to the west blood red where the sun had gone" (232–33). Many such small details reward a close reading.

The color blue takes on ominous meaning when it is associated with the "blue walls and a single blue bulb" in the corridor leading to Eduardo's office (130) and his "sleek oiled head blue in the light" during the knifefight (248). The truckload of Mexicans helped by Billy are silhouetted against the "deep burnt cobalt of the sky" (33). The cabdriver who hails John Grady while he is searching for Magdalena has "a blue suit of polished serge" and an umbrella with a sheet of "blue cellophane," under which "the driver's face was blue" (55). As John Grady and Mr. Johnson discuss the topic of marriage, the sky turns "dark and blue" (187). When Billy helps John Grady paint the old mountain shack with an ugly bright blue, he unwittingly symbolizes Eduardo's ownership of his dream (179). When Magdalena flees the hospital by running out into the dangerous streets of Juárez, she seeks "some favored inclination in the blue light of the desert stars by which she would stand revealed for who she truly was" (210). But the stars hold no such promise, as their blueness symbolizes Eduardo's possession. On the morning of her death, Magdalena hopefully puts on a blue dress and regards "herself in the dimly lit mirror" (219), like a doomed Virgin of Guadalupe: the cab that arrives at the café—the one in which Magdalena unknowingly rides to meet Tiburcio instead of John Grady—is also painted blue. Blue portends the disaster in Mexico, a blue corridor leading to Eduardo. In the end, as Billy carries John Grady's body in his arms through the streets in the "gray Monday dawn," a group of schoolchildren "dressed in blue uniforms" witness the lonely funeral procession and bless themselves in "gray light" (261).

The colors green and gray represent, respectively, the dreams of John Grady juxtaposed with grim reality. Like F. Scott Fitzgerald's use of a green beacon in *The Great Gatsby,* green symbolizes John Grady's hopes for a better life. This color's first association with John Grady's dreams is implied in the description of the "live belt of green" that runs down the Rio Grande valley, contrasted with the "fenced gray fields" and "gray dust" of the "gray furrows" (10–11). Gray is the absence of life in a dead landscape seen close up. McCarthy doubles images of the cold grayness of dawn throughout the novel. In Juárez, the gutters run with "a grayish water" (7), and in the White Lake, in the "gray light" of a new day, the tattered reality of the whorehouse becomes apparent: "stains on the carpet, worn places on the arms of the furniture, cigarette burns" (71). In contrast, at night the cities on the plain appear so pretty, deceptively scintillating "like a tiara laid out upon a jeweler's blackcloth" (87). The word *tiara* is also used to describe the chandelier in the White Lake, connecting the glittering lights of the city with the glass lights of the brothel (67). The beckoning "aura of the lights" is beautiful (78), but in the grayness of day, one can see more clearly: "The desert plain lay cold and blue below them in the graying light and the shape of the river running down from the north through the break of gray winter trees lay in the pale serpentine of mist. To the south the cold gray grid of the distant city and the shape of the older city across the river like stampings in the desert soil" (92). Notice that in the cold light of day, the desert also reveals the ominous blueness associated with Eduardo. From high in the upper range, Billy and John Grady see the "thin standing spire of smoke . . . rising vertically in the still blue morning air" and Billy remarks how it looks "different from up here. Always looked different. It was different" (216). The American cowboys' idealistic dreams of the "green line of the river breaks" is lost in the "pale serpentine of mist" (92) and "range on range the distant mountains of Mexico" (217) signifying a "future unknown" (195). All the pretty lights of the city at night contrast with the squalid "cold gray grid" of the streets by day (92). McCarthy extends the symbolism by showing John Grady with his arm around a bloody dog with "four bloody furrows along her flank" that has returned to camp "bearing witness to things they could only imagine or suppose out there in the night" (91). The dog's bloody furrows hearken back to the description of the landscape's gray furrows, which also foreshadow Eduardo's four bloody cuts spelling out the letter E in John Grady's thigh during the knifefight (252). Likewise, as Magdalena leaves the White Lake for the last time, the city lights are described as a breathtaking reflection of the heavens, "burning on the plain like stars pooled in a lake" (221). The illusion of beauty here is undercut by the word *pooled,* which has echoes in the autumn pools of dead leaves (27) and the "pools of rainwater" during the knifefight (247).

When John Grady and Billy look out over the surrounding countryside from high in the upper range of the Jarillas, they see the "green of the benchland below" and the "thin straight line of the highway and a toysized truck" and the "green line of the river breaks" (216–17). The first night he makes love to Magdalena, John Grady notices the light running like "a river over her naked shoulders," connecting the green of the river to his dream of true love (69). Yet on the first page of the novel, McCarthy has already intimated the end of the green dream in the bleeding of green neon. When Magdalena awakens from her epileptic fit on the steel table, she runs out through a "gray metal door" (208) and escapes through a "long green corridor dimly lit and stretching away to a closed door at the end" (209). Her fate is thus sealed symbolically by the grayness of the door as a harsh reality closing off the green corridor of love. The day of Magdalena's death, John Grady rides into the high country one more time and contemplates the lonely landscape: "To the south the thin green line of the river lay like a child's crayon mark across that mauve and bistre waste. Beyond that the mountains of Mexico in paling blues and grays washing out in the distance" (230). The "crayon mark" and "mauve" (230) echo the description of Magdalena's "painted child's mouth" (67) and the naïve childishness of John Grady's romantic dream. The thin green line of love is reflected in the landscape as youthful desire, another kind of idealistic "picturebook" (*All the Pretty Horses* 16), an impossible dream when faced with the "paling blues and grays washing out in the distance" (230).

Yellow and red, white and blue, gray and green, circles and webs, night and day, reflections and blindness—all these thematic motifs are carefully woven into the novel's overlapping images, forming a densely figurative tapestry. The color yellow connects the mirror in La Venada, the "yellowing glass of the old Brunswick backbar" (5), to the "yellow leaves" that "turn and drift in a pool" (27), to Magdalena's yellow lamplight (100), to "the yellow bulb screwed into the fixture over the back door" (78), to the "yellowed finger" of the blind man (81). The yellow associations all point to the false hopes engendered by John Grady's ardent green love for Magdalena. The green leaves turn yellow in the fall, where they end up dying in the pool, which is doubled in the black pools of rainwater outside the White Lake on the night of the knifefight. On his way to get some answers from Eduardo, Billy stands under a "green and yellowed tiled arch" (236), which in McCarthy's arcane encoding gestures toward the disastrous mixture of green dreams and yellow deceptions. The morning after the knifefight, as John Grady lies dying of his wounds, Billy sets out to find help: "As he trotted out across the vacant lot he looked back. The square of yellow light that shone through the sacking looked like some haven of promise out there on the shore of the breaking world but his heart misgave him" (260). It is too late. In the "gray dawn" the "stars had dimmed out and the dark shapes of the mountains stood along the sky" (261). The false hopes of yellow and the glittering promise of stars fade into the gray morning of a grim Mexican reality. When Billy returns a few minutes later, John Grady is dead.

The blind pianist, like so many of McCarthy's anchorites, offers vague, misleading advice: "You must persevere. To persevere is everything" (81). While this kind of simple idealism appeals to John Grady's stubborn machismo, which drives him to follow his heart and never give up—on a horse or a woman—it is bad advice, especially given the ominous context of the next lines:

> My belief is that she is at best a visitor. At best. She does not belong here.
> Among us.
> Yessir. I know she don't belong here.
> No, said the blind man. I do not mean in this house. I mean here. Among us. (81–82)

John Grady gives no clue that he understands what the blind man has just intimated: that he and Magdalena will soon die. John Grady walks back "carrying the blind man's words concerning his prospects as if they were a contract with the world to come," yet he is unable to act on the truth he has been told (82). Later, when John Grady asks the blind man to stand in as Magdalena's godfather, the blind man refuses because he believes that Eduardo will kill her. At this revelation, John Grady demands that the blind man tell him what to do. Instead he is given a strangely direct yet evasive riddle: "You must understand. I have no certainty. And it is a grave matter" (197). The word *grave* works as a double entendre to signify that in the course of the world's events the matter is already settled. Magdalena will die. At the end of this conversation, McCarthy uses a dialogue between John Grady and the blind man as a direct expression of his theme:

> You think I'm a fool.
> No. I do not.
> You would not say so if you did.
> No, but I would not lie. I don't think it. I never did. A man is always right to pursue the thing he loves.
> No matter even it if kills him?
> I think so. Yes. No matter even that. (199)

But this is an impossible outcome for the youth to accept. All of his success in life has been improbable and hard-earned—training horses, chasing wild dogs, fighting in Mexico. He gives no quarter to the possibility of failure. On the ranch, his honesty and determination have paid rich dividends, garnering him the respect of other men in the region. His refusal to give up on the "owlheaded" colt leads Billy to predict, "I got a suspicion that whatever it is he aims to do he'll most likely get it done" (14). When John Grady alertly spots that a horse is lame in the right foreleg and won't allow delivery, he has to stand firm against another man's insistent prodding that he take the horse anyway. Six times John Grady firmly denies the man's request, and the incident almost escalates into a fight (46–47). But the owner of the injured horse is so impressed by John Grady's keen judgment that he tries to hire the young man, full-time or part-time, whatever he can get. Billy, the voice of reason, tells him to do it, that it's a good deal, but John Grady's loyalty to Mac is like his loyalty to horses and women. He will work for only one man at a time. Once he's made up his mind, he never quits a horse. In a clash of wills, John Grady always stands firm, true to his word according to his best judgment. This quality can be admirable and, at times, can make the difference between failure and success. In the dog hunt, John Grady leads the way on a precarious route to the top of the mesa by tying his jacket over the horse's head to calm it (166). Here again, blinding the horse takes on thematic overtones, connecting with John Grady's willingness to go to any lengths to succeed, even if it means self-imposed blindness. Going into Juárez to make love to Magdalena and planning a future with her is another kind of blind deception, one he is unwilling to admit when confronted by older voices of reason. After the rousing dog hunt, when John Grady and Billy go back after the pups only to discover an unmovable boulder on top of the den, John Grady is the one who won't give up. With great effort and at his own peril, he rigs an impromptu lever and winch to tip the boulder over (174–76). And it works. Through sheer determination and quick wits, John Grady wins the day.

But the night is a different story. When he insists on pursuing unorthodox, extreme measures at night, he becomes as foolish as those frozen jackrabbits. One night after spraining an ankle, John Grady wakes everyone on the ranch with a crazy attempt to train the colt in the middle of the night. Billy upbraids him, asking, "What the hell's got into you? . . . You can't even see to rope the son of a bitch," and Oren labels it all a "bunch of damned ignorance" (17–18). John Grady, however, is not chastened and only replies, "It wasnt any of your business" (19). The phrase "son of a bitch" and the inability to see constitute additional links with blindness, the faulty light switch, and the peculiar coyote as other unnatural events. Another incident demonstrating John Grady's fallibility at night is his loss of a chess game to Mac, a player whom he usually beats during the daytime. When Billy asks John Grady if he slacked up "on him just the littlest bit," he answers "No. I don't believe in it" (93). John Grady never quits, never changes his mind, never slacks up, not even a little bit.

John Grady's penchant for always standing his ground adheres to the manly code of the Old West. Thus it is not surprising that he finds common ground with Mr. Johnson, the old cowboy. Mr. Johnson also wakes up others with crazy antics in the night, and it is John Grady who goes out to get the old man, who is dressed only in his hat and boots and a "long white unionsuit . . . like the ghost of some ancient waddy wandering there" (104). John Grady defends the old man's behavior, ignoring Billy's comment "That's pitiful" and telling Mac, "He aint loony. He's just old" (104–6). Noticing that John Grady and the old man "have a lot in common," Billy warns the boy to not "be hangin around him so much" (127). But John Grady enjoys listening to Mr. Johnson's stories of the Old West, tales about going on cattle drives to Abilene and, suitably enough, of once being shot at while bringing some "stolen horses we'd recovered" out of Mexico (63), mirroring John Grady's experiences in *All the Pretty Horses*.

One of McCarthy's persistent themes in the western novels is the certainty of dark fate. Although his characters are unaware of what the future holds, McCarthy's last sentence in the main text of *Cities of the Plain* returns to determinism: " . . . the woman stepped once more into the street and the children followed and all continued on to their appointed places which as some believe were chosen long ago even to the beginning of the world" (262). The circle motif represents chosen paths as closed orbits. McCarthy's symbolism here departs from traditional understanding of the circle as a representation of eternity—as in the wedding ring, the stone circles of England, and the Aztecs' calendar, *la Piedra del Sol*. The clocklike circles of the sun and moon arching across the dome of sky have long suggested celestial eternity. However, McCarthy uses circle images to indicate the inscribed birth and death of each individual. In *Blood*

Meridian, the "tethered coin" of one's life is destined by an invisible string to fly out into the night and, at a designated time, to return again into the hand of an appointed death. In *Cities of the Plain,* circle images especially predominate in the description of a young man's funeral, as witnessed by Magdalena after she has seen John Grady for the last time. The scene strikes her as a terrifying epiphany of coming tragedy, causing her to collapse into an epileptic fit:

> The cart rattled past and the spoked wheels diced slowly the farther streetside and the solemn watchers there, a cardfan of sorted faces under the shopfronts and the long skeins of light in the street broken in the turning spokes and the shadows of the horses tramping upright and oblique before the oblong shadows of the wheels shaping over the stones and turning and turning. (208)

The young man, pale and newly dead, of course prefigures John Grady's fate, something made more clear by the ominous presence of the "blind maestro" (207). Later in the night Magdalena tells a woman, "in three days' time the boy she loved would come to marry her," suggesting the promise of a risen savior, a Christ (211). But the turning wheels of the funeral cart are full of the closed lines inscribing only circles within circles. Within the circles there is no promise of an afterlife, no Christ, no salvation, no other possibility except certain death. Even the straight shafts of light are caught and broken in the brutal fate of the wheels' circling, "turning and turning" (208). The circle image is also seen in the face of the clock in Mac's house, which McCarthy carefully describes at several points in the narrative. After a conversation about marriage, John Grady sits pondering the horizon: "Through the window far to the south he could see the thin white adderstongues of lightning licking silently along the rim of the sky in the darkness over Mexico. The only sound was the clock ticking in the hallway" (203). The clock's loud ticking at night is the sound of time passing, regulated and parceled into small, discrete units. The ticking, like the hands of the clock sweeping around in circles, is immutable fate, a future already decided. John Grady hears the ticking sound again in his dream of the young girl dead on a "palletboard like a sacrificial virgin," describing it as a "periodic click like a misset metronome, a clock, a portent. A measure of something periodic and otherwise silent and vastly patient which only darkness could accommodate"(104). The deadliness of circles is finally made evident in Eduardo's circular motions during the knifefight, as McCarthy uses the terms *circled* or *circling* no less than seventeen times (248–53). McCarthy's interconnecting symbols are woven so tightly into his descriptions that one begins to notice a complex web of thematic motifs embedded in almost every line.

McCarthy's use of thematic motif is perhaps most noticeable in the novel's frequent references to mirrors. John Grady first sees Magdalena framed in a yellow "backbar glass" (6), a beautiful girl with downcast eyes and long black hair that she sweeps back as he watches; later, at the White Lake, he repeatedly looks for her in the "glass of the backbar" (66). At first he sees only the reflection of "a tall woman in a diaphanous gown," who looks like "a ghost of a whore" (66). This small detail is doubled later in Magdalena's half-crazed night journey through the dangerous streets of Juárez, when she is wearing only a sheer white shift. At one point the car lights cast "her slight figure up onto the walls in enormous dark transparency with the shift burned away and the bones all but showing" and further on "in the glare of the headlights" she appears "like some tattered phantom routed out of the ordinal dark and hounded briefly through the visible world to vanish again into the history of men's dreams" (209–10). The danger of the onrushing headlights in Juárez also hearkens back to the unfortunate jackrabbits and the owl accident, with its image of "an enormous moth in a web" (34), an image that is reinforced here by the mention of "a millermoth that patrolled [a lightbulb] in random clockwise orbits" (208). With only enough money to buy a drink at the White Lake, John Grady keeps an eye on Magdalena by watching her in the bar mirror and thinks perhaps "she had been watching him" (85). In another mirror, the one-eyed criada and Josefina look at Magdalena critically. Here McCarthy takes great care to denote the difference between the real girl and the mirror's image:

> She [Josefina] studied the girl and she studied the girl in the mirror. The criada had stepped back and stood holding the brush in both hands. She and Josefina studied the girl in the mirror, the three of them in the yellow light of the tablelamp standing there within

the gilded plaster scrollwork of the mirror's frame like figures in an antique flemish painting. (100)

In thematic terms, this passage's reiteration of the words *mirror* and *girl* juxtaposes reality with the false reflections of hope. Because the two images, one real and the other unreal, tend to look alike, the two attending women check back and forth to make sure of their handiwork. What they see in the mirror is a pretty picture framed in gold. And it is this pretty, false mirror image that dominates the scene, lending the picture a gilt-edged unreality. As Magdalena continues to stare at herself in the mirror, the woman's eye winks "in suggestive complicity," an unnatural sign which, like the faulty taillight, foretells a tragic end.

Unlike John Grady, however, Magdalena is not so easily fooled by the false hopes of the pretty mirror image. When the criada suggests the fantasy of marrying a rich man and living in a fine house with beautiful children, the girl does not answer.

> She looked across the old woman's shoulder into the eyes in the glass as if it were some sister there who weathered stoically this beleaguerment of her hopes. Standing in the gaudy boudoir that was itself a tawdry emulation of other rooms, other worlds. Regarding her own false arrogance in the pierglass as if it were proof against the old woman's entreaties, the old woman's promises. Standing like some maid in a fable spurning the offerings of the hag which do conceal within them unspoken covenants of corruption. Claims that can never be quit, estates forever entailed. She spoke to that girl standing in the glass and she said that one could not know where it was that one had taken the path one was upon but only that one was upon it. (101)

At times, this storybook Cinderella clearly sees the harsh reality of her world. Her epileptic convulsions, which the other women consider sacred, the divine touch of God, are moments of deathly clarity, in which she is literally seized by the violent, bloody truth of her coming demise. In the conversation with the criada, the old woman is puzzled by the talk of life's paths, and Magdalena explains simply, "Cualquier senda. Esta senda. La senda que escoja," which translates, "Any path. This path. The path that is chosen" (101). Unlike John Grady, who lives in the bright green world of the American ranch, a cowboy paradise, Magdalena is a woman of the night, a prescient owl who understands her blue destiny, her tragically closed circle of fate. She wants to believe in John Grady because she loves him, yet she remains a figure of pathos, one who knows about the unreality of gilded reflections.

Reflections appear throughout the novel. Eduardo's office has a desk of "polished glass" and "a low coffeetable of glass and chrome," which resemble the reflections from Tiburcio's "greased hair" and the "glossy sheen" of his black shirt (79). Yet the shiny blackness of Tiburcio contrasts with the clean white leather couch and cream-colored carpet of Eduardo's furnishings. The implication is that Eduardo and Tiburcio are twinned images of each other, alike in their deceptive reflections yet different in social status. As the boss, Eduardo fancies himself a businessman who has risen cleanly above the greasy dealings of his henchman, who has the base duty of working directly with the whores and collecting money from customers. But this illusion ends on the night of the knifefight, when Eduardo's head glistens blue with oil, like Tiburcio's, even as he complains that he should be past "fighting in alleys with knives" (249).

Small moments in the novel work as thematic motifs. When Billy goes to the White Lake to gauge Eduardo's reaction to John Grady's proposal to buy Magdalena, he likewise watches the women in the backbar mirror and is suddenly startled by Tiburcio, who materializes "standing at his left elbow like Lucifer" (128). When Billy takes a cab ride while investigating John Grady's disappearance, the cabdriver looks at him in the mirror (236), which would be innocent enough except for the connecting detail of the cabdriver's watching Magdalena in the mirror on her death ride (225). At the White Lake, as John Grady looks for Magdalena in the "glass of the backbar," a cockroach creeps up the counter of the bar, in between the bottles, and ascends "to the glass where it encountered itself and froze" (66). The cockroach is fooled by its own false image and, like the jackrabbits, freezes in an intractable position. John Grady likewise fails to question the false reflections in the mirror. In the directness of the daylight, out in the raw elements of nature, he is a true cowboy hero, a strong-willed man, the best hand on the ranch. He never second-guesses his judgment concerning horses or wild dogs. He stubbornly stays with his plan to get the boulder off the pups' den. Once he has made a decision—and all of his decisions are spontaneous and from the heart—he stands by it until the end. But at night, across the border in Juárez, in the glittering world of mirrors, blue cabs, and one alluring girl, he is out of his element. John Grady's unshakeable sense of his own infallibility is more than a stubborn streak—it is the fatal flaw that undoes all of the green dreams of his ranch paradise.

Readers of *Cities of the Plain* will soon notice a structural anomaly setting this novel apart from McCarthy's previous westerns: the permanence of its locale. The characters are no longer nomadic, and the action remains centered around Mac's ranch and the whorehouses of Juárez. In particular, John Grady has set down roots and has plans for staying on at Mac's ranch for the duration. The looming possibility of an army takeover of the property hints at the impermanence of this position; in fact, Mr. Johnson guesses that eventually the army will take "the whole Tularosa basin" (62). But the main characters, like John Grady in Mexico, remain oblivious to this fate. Until the army takeover, they will persist. This novel's uncharacteristic permanence of locale strengthens the narrative in a couple of ways: first, by demonstrating how much John Grady has to lose, and second, by juxtaposing the peaceful dream of pastoralism against the violence of Mexico. John Grady's green pastoral dream of happiness has already been half-fulfilled. In a way, he has recouped many of the losses incurred in *All the Pretty Horses*. He is no longer haunted by memories of Alejandra or the deaths of Blevins, the inmate, and the Mexican captain. His position on the ranch as a favored son of Mr. Johnson and Mac has given him another chance to have paternal authority figures. His respect for Mr. Johnson equals the respect he had as a boy for his pioneering grandfather, who, like Mr. Johnson, survived the dangers of the frontier. And Mac is even more suitable as a surrogate father than his real father had ever been. Mac willingly offers advice, plays chess, loans money, and admires John Grady's horsemanship. All John Grady needs to complete this version of the American Eden is an Eve. But this is where, once again, he rejects all advice and falls into hubris—precisely the original sin he had been guilty of at Don Hector's hacienda in *All the Pretty Horses*. There also, John Grady established himself as a top hand, a man who knew and loved horses; there also he risked everything for the love of Eve. With both Alejandra and Magdalena, however, he fails to devise a workable plan of action and pays the price in a knifefight. In *All the Pretty Horses,* he wins by killing the inmate and thus lives to dream again. In this novel the hubris proves tragic in a classical sense and is therefore fatal.

The cowboy hero, in all his pastoral glory, decidedly qualifies as an American version of the noble figure worthy of tragedy. Although John Grady is not royal in an Aristotelian sense, he meets the larger-than-life requirements of the tragic hero with his status as the best hand on the ranch. As the primary icon in the American pantheon of heroes, the cowboy represents the quintessential man. John Grady's simple dream of fixing up the shack for his Mexican bride replays the pioneer's dream of forging a garden-paradise in the wilderness; as in *All the Pretty Horses,* McCarthy offers a version of the western myth of progress. With Magdalena by his side and a steady position on Mac's ranch, John Grady would have everything he needs. But this everything, this potential happiness, is doomed from the moment he chooses Magdalena as his Eve by a fatal paradox: Magdalena is controlled not by God but by Eduardo, and to oppose Eduardo inevitably means to lose Magdalena.

By restricting the narrative to Mac's ranch and Juárez, McCarthy has come full circle: the end of the trail is its beginning. The protagonists of *Blood Meridian* and the Border Trilogy represent the American wanderlust for adventure, the whole westering manifesto that promises so much and serves as the centerpiece of American mythos. We all have felt the mythic impulse for heroics: to love, to rebel, to get back to nature, to stake out turf, to build a little place we can call our own. But if such dreams fed the pioneering of the West, they are certainly not the whole of reality, not the entire history. In reality, the Old West was often a violent and lawless place of massacres and Darwinian "right by might," the Old West of *Blood Meridian*. In the Border Trilogy, McCarthy's vision of Mexico embodies the violence of the Old West. Mexico is the glittering night dream of adventure and a gray land of death. The hard lessons of McCarthy's westerns teach us that the green hopes of youthful dreams— all the pretty horses, Alejandra, the she-wolf, Blevins, Boyd, the scintillating lights of the cities, Magdalena in the mirror—are fanciful chimeras, mere reflections in the night, the artifice of lamps and neon, which bleed and die in a gray dawn.

Afterword

Still,
I would leap too
Into the light,
If I had the chance,
It is everything, the wet green stalk of the field
On the other side of the road.
—James Wright,
from "Small Frogs Killed on the Highway"

The dramatic shift from the mindless violence of *Blood Meridian* to the pastoral dreams of *All the Pretty Horses* parallels America's shift away from the pessimism of Vietnam. The cultural memory of fifty-eight thousand American deaths from that conflict is fading, and for the young it never existed. Many students nowadays are hard-pressed to distinguish between World War II, Korea, and Vietnam. They are wars from long ago fought for reasons mostly forgotten. During the Gulf War and the war in Yugoslavia, politicians and generals, some of whom were soldiers in Vietnam, remembered the differences between those wars and determined to keep American casualties to a minimum. As the world's premier military power at century's end, our nation still followed Teddy Roosevelt's advice to "speak softly and carry a big stick," yet quite often we used the big stick. We began the century mired in a dirty little war, cracked the back of our political and economic might with two dirty little wars in Korea and Vietnam, and, at century's end, were again entangled by doing the right thing in the Middle East and the Balkans. Inevitably, there were repercussions that prove that one of the fundamental laws of physics also applies to history: for every action, there must be an equal reaction. The aftershocks of Vietnam continue as thousands of veterans struggle with physical and psychological wounds. Many are homeless; many have committed suicide.

In a strange way, the rise of our high-octane, media pop-culture parallels the vets' agony. Like a national post-traumatic stress disorder, postmodernism in all its adrenaline-rush glory is like a patch, a drink, a fix, a recurring nightmare. It is Hamburger Hill, the Tet Offensive, My Lai, and Kent State come back to haunt us. The Kubrick-Lynch-Stone-Tarantino weird pastiche of the old ultraviolence is ultracool and surreal. It enthralls with the sensational. Its thrills are iconoclastic and unconventional. Its rush is hilarious, zany, and utterly insane. The big grin of postmodernism, the sardonic wit of Stephen Crane, the rueful laughter of Jack London, the enigmatic smile of Cormac McCarthy's Judge Holden. And in the real world there is nothing funny about it.

On a recent trip to New York City, I took the requisite tourist boat out to the Statue of Liberty. Along with feelings of awe for the history of America's immigrants and the inspiration of Miss Liberty's torch, I was struck by New York's vulnerability. In person, Miss Liberty looks smaller than on TV. Like a rusting hood ornament, she represents freedom, the hopes and dreams of previous generations. But to outsiders, she's a target of opportunity, representing the aggressive power of America's fiscal and military might worldwide. She offers a prime target for any terrorist with a grudge and a briefcase. At century's end, the national paranoia of the Cold War had been transformed into national paranoia over Third World terrorism. Each act of terrorism confirms our elephantine fears of the Third World mouse. The next time, we fear, might prove more serious—a nuclear backpack, a briefcase full of anthrax.

Ultimately all violence is primal and self-destructive. That is the lesson of Vietnam and the lesson of *Blood Meridian*. Returning to pleasant green dreams of progress myths is not going to solve current problems. Myths can only mask the brutal nature of reality, cloak them with cultural meanings. For those who are in the midst of violence, the truth, as Tim O'Brien remarks, "is never moral."

> A true war story is never moral. It does not instruct, nor encourage virtue, nor suggest models of proper human behavior, nor restrain

men from doing the things men have always done. If a story seems moral, do not believe it. If at the end of a war story you feel uplifted, or if you feel that some small bit of rectitude has been salvaged from the larger waste, then you have been made the victim of a very old and terrible lie. There is no rectitude whatsoever. There is no virtue. (O'Brien 76)

War is the old story of one race killing another—in ageless reenactment of what Hegel called "bloody battle." By inventing popular heroes who regress to redeem, who commit acts of sacred violence, we risk everything. Our trigger finger of national security becomes insecurity as we seek to maintain interests abroad without bloodshed as well as to protect our middle-class comforts at home. Empires engender wars, but so does every other kind of political arrangement, from bands to tribes to federations to nations. What myths don't tell us is that death is usually not sacrificial or redemptive or sacred. And heroes don't always win. America will continue to be a vulnerable target. Our best efforts to control unstable foreign powers are doomed. The chaos of international conflicts involves us in ancient animosities of race, religion, and politics. Sooner or later, as Thomas Jefferson warned two hundred years ago, foreign disputes lead to "entangling alliances" and escalation. Small conflicts become wars.

At home First Man will continue to threaten our middle-class comforts. We all want our children to feel safe at night and to wake up the next morning without the threats of nuclear bombs or anthrax or shotguns in the back alley. But their future may not be secure. When Judge Holden gestures toward the Anasazi ruins and describes them as the end result of empire building, he prophesies America's future. The lessons of history, especially from the twentieth century, have been contradictory and uncertain. The two world wars knocked down old empires and gave America an opportunity to build a new one. Since the mid-forties it has been our turn to create a new world, another "city on a hill." And what have we done with it? In a democratic country of well-educated philosopher-kings, we have elected leaders with imprecise, short-term foreign policies laden with vague entry-exit scenarios. Politicians still employ frontier myths as slick rhetoric to sell American ideals. Instead of becoming a model society, we have wasted time squabbling. In taking the low road, we have taken the one much traveled. The postmodern media game of mindless violence leads to general malaise and specific horrific events such as the massacre at Columbine High School. Of the thousands of commentators speculating on the motives of the two teenagers responsible, a retired special-ops colonel may have been the most accurate in discussing the parallels between the boys' obsession with Doom and Wargasm and his own soldiers' professional training using the same two video games.

Although America is at "the peak of its achievement," Judge Holden warns us, "the noon of his expression signals the onset of night" (146–47). The twentieth century may be most remembered for its wars of genocide, the stockpiling of weapons of mass destruction, global environmental devastation, and an uncontrolled population explosion. If the cogs of the Information Age ever grind to a halt in one of a thousand possible scenarios, societies may quickly revert to atavism. In some places they already have. And then the apocalyptic world of *Blood Meridian* won't seem so very shocking. McCarthy does not offer us any easy answers or qualify *Blood Meridian*'s violence with platitudes or comforting endings. Instead his prose compels us to read on, to turn the next page, to face the next killing. As witnesses, we struggle in a vortex of desire and restraint: "This is too awful, but what a sight!" The text answers questions we would rather not ask. We want to wish away evil logic, to reach instead for the security of mythic conventions and heroic figures. *Blood Meridian* does not allow us this luxury. How can we ignore the daily headlines with their real violence? How can we ignore the real violence we encounter in the streets? How can we live with the highest murder rate of any nation in a state of peace? The enduring problem of *Blood Meridian* is the historical yet contemporary accuracy of its theme.

Yet, like most Americans, McCarthy himself turns away from the horrible truths of *Blood Meridian*. In the Border Trilogy, the Adamic figure is resurrected to be crucified once again. The popularity of these westerns informs us that frontier myths have not been permanently set aside or fundamentally altered by the unpopular war in Vietnam. Like James Wright's tadpoles swimming under a silvery moon, the young are waiting—waiting and dreaming—for that great and shining moment when they too may leap into the air and soar.

AFTERWORD

A Parable:
Notes from the Annual Conference of the Association of Literary Scholars and Critics

Outside the hotel, with a roll of thin wire wrapped around his left arm, unspooling down around his feet in tangled heaps—Hobbes's First Man in rags, an anchorite methodically winding, unwinding, winding, breathing heavily, half-muttering an old Doors song, "Strange! When you're strange, people are strangers, people are strange, women are wicked, women are ugly, Strange! when you're strange." His lips press out each word like a mantra, while his mind, his mind, is off somewhere else, bingeing on faraway dreams. His hands frantically pull out wire in short bursts, then with quick wrists snap it like a whiplash in the sun, a deft maneuver really, something he learned in 'Nam. Winding, unwinding, jerk-snap, another neck twisted, just like chickens, snap, snap, "zero at the bone."

Inside the hotel, an eminent scholar, somewhat boorish in rumpled corduroy, a rich man gone sidewise into academe and now useless to the family fortune, frumpy, dour, drooping, but a great American scholar nonetheless, mumbles his way through a paper, ambagious, amphigory, an amicus curiae, droning on and on something about the craft of poetry and its need—yea, verily, the need of western literature itself, the whole rumpled literary opus, the sacred cow canon, for a new cultural dialectic, a post-post-structuralism, a neo-something, a universal critical theory of everything since the old Marxists, the waxy deconstructionists, the pensioned New Critics, the aging young Turks of semiotics, the rainbow coalition of minorities, feminists and gays, Blacks and Chicanos, Asians and Native Americans, all the assorted schools and agendas, which always acknowledge up front their particular geopolitical positions, their particular bias of academic discourse—all just aren't as convincing anymore, too seventies-passé. The scope of cultural studies has narrowed into camps, piecemeal, gauche, driven by polemics, and my God, it's a war zone out there, atavistic even, all the mean backbiting and infighting dividing departments, so inelegant, so graceless, and all so unpoetic, really.

In the foyer, next to a shiny silver coffeepot, a dirty homeless woman, an anile old crone, half-muttering, reaches a bony hand out for a croissant as a security guard quietly arrives to escort her out.

Outside, the fevered brain of the well-wired First Man ponders its own verities, then snap, another head rolls, more wire, another loop, a grimace, almost beatific, a lizard smile of admonition, rocking, a genuflection. One of the hotel doormen, a small fat man dressed like Harlequin in navy blue with gold fringe, an overstuffed pincushion of authority, moves in, takes charge, insolent and rude, "Okay, that's enough, move on, now, let's move on!" Not much, but enough of this for about a minute, when out of his crouch, spastic First Man lurches, jerking out his wire, primal, reptilian, crocodilic, snap, snap. The sharp metallic zing slices clean, missing the doorman's head by half a foot. Ah, aging reflexes to be sure, but witness the pure fury of it! So full of simple intent, so concentrated and neat, the graceful, murderous lunge. And the little fat doorman, an organ-grinder's monkey, surprised, falls back, stumbling, funny, grotesque, desperate, crawling on all fours to escape the pursuing wire—zing, zing, snap, snap. What saves him, certainly, is First Man's age, perhaps drugs, alcohol, hunger, insanity, disease, yes, probably. This fifty-year-old homeless vet just doesn't have it anymore. He's lost his touch. After a few feet he stumbles away, bewildered and irritated, declaiming, "Goddamn you, motherfucker, you motherfucker!"

Inside, inspired now by his own rambling erudition, the poet-scholar, a Last Man in full dotage, forgets his prepared comments and aspires, ad hoc, toward a new literary theory of everything, a universal poetics, diacritical and dialectical. But there's something more, something more tangible, something about American scholars in cloudy aeries, their Laputan love for rebarbative razzmatazz. It is time to find other voices, new resonances—say, from sociobiology, the new ethology and its compelling evidence for apes in the family of man, Hominidae, and the great migration "out of Africa." There might be something there, perhaps, a synthesis of Hobbes, Rousseau, Hegel, Nietzsche, along with the ideas of Morris, Wilson, Washburn and Lancaster, Diamond, Dawkins with his memes. Maybe recycle the old Man as Hunter once more, mixing in Ehrenreich's ideas on Man the Hunted, some Fukuyama, Huntington,

AFTERWORD

Kaplan, Wrangham and Peterson, something akin to the naturalism of London and Crane. Yes, it might be done along these lines, most certainly. Neo-naturalism, it has a nice ring.

Down the escalator, on the mezzanine level, inside a men's restroom, in a stall, an anonymous street artist scrawls, "EAT SHIT!"

Outside, the police arrive but the tramp has moved on, ubiquitous, invisible on every street corner, with cardboard signs proclaiming "For God So Loved," "God Bless," or "It's for Beer." The mayor, elected on a promise to clean up the streets, started with litter and now wants to clean up the homeless, to move them on—so begins the organized hassle. Bus drivers, security guards, doormen, police, everyone wants them to just move on. And they do, all the way, at least at nights, to Golden Gate Park, some alone, some in huddled bands, cold, diseased, depressed, insane, drugged, drunk, desperate, and their lives are brutish and short. But they are out there, in the dark, with wire, knives, and guns, mindless and angry, waiting for first light.

On the way to the airport, the cabby—a cyberpunk, disheveled, pierced and tattooed—raves on about mass destruction, Mission District bookstores, how his racehorse never came in, the coming fall of civilization, social collapse, the redistribution, Revelations, nuclear Armageddon, AIDS, Y2K, the millennium, what it is like to be on the outside looking in, and what will happen when the "whole shithouse goes up in flames."

November 1997
San Francisco
Toward a New Literary Theory

Notes

Introduction

1. The useful phrase "historical bedrock" is appropriated from Patricia Limerick's *The Legacy of Conquest,* which states, "Conquest forms the historical bedrock of the whole nation" (27).

2. *Blood Meridian,* p. 116. The judge affirms that God does not lie by holding up a "chunk of rock" and proclaiming, "these are his words. . . . He speaks in stones and trees, the bones of things."

3. *Blood Meridian,* p. 130. The ex-priest Tobin is describing Glanton's gang after they encounter the judge.

4. The most popular on-line site for McCarthy fans as of 1999 was The Cormac McCarthy Society at www.cormacmccarthy.com.

5. The useful term "moveable feast" has been used since the middle ages to describe a holiday whose calendar date varies from year to year. Perhaps with a nod to Ernest Hemingway, who chose it as the title of his autobiography, historians like Patricia Nelson Limerick and Susan Armitage have employed the phrase to describe pioneering in the American West.

6. The phrase "fatal environment" was originally coined by Walt Whitman after Custer's Last Stand to describe conditions in the West. Richard Slotkin has used it as the title of his second study of western myths in American culture, *The Fatal Environment* (New York: Atheneum, 1985).

7. McCarthy's prose style can be traced back to various sources. His dialogue and action sequences are minimal like Hemingway's, while his narrative descriptions are expansive and poetic like Faulkner's. For more information on McCarthy's style, see Nancy Kreml's "Stylistic Variation and Cognitive Constraint in *All the Pretty Horses.*"

Chapter 2.
Blood Meridian and the Reassessment of Violence

1. René Girard's *Violence and the Sacred* discusses containing violence within well-established social rituals. The consequences of lawless violence are like a contagious disease. Once begun, violence can easily spread and become epidemic, spilling over in unexpected ways to other parts of society. The war in Vietnam became a Girardian contagion of violence in American society. Antiwar protestors joined forces with civil-rights and environmental groups to demonstrate against a broad range of social ills. Extremists pushed beyond protest into acts of nihilistic terror. The war in Vietnam spawned an escalating cycle of violence, including riots and bombings, reproduced in graphic media coverage.

2. Richard Slotkin's *Regeneration through Violence* is the first of a trilogy of works exploring frontier violence. The title accurately summarizes one of Slotkin's chief ideas: that Americans have long sought violence in frontier regions as a way to further American ideals and to experience national catharses.

3. The offhand remark about "no God in Mexico" recalls a 1970s-era country-western song by Billy Joe Shaver, "Ain't No God in Mexico," a reference McCarthy employs again in *Cities of the Plain:* "In Mexico there is no God" (116).

4. Hollon notes that "not one of the 370 treaties made with the Indians since 1789 has been kept by the federal government" (124) and that "hatred of the Indian began before the first English settler reached American soil" (125). He claims there were 1,243 battles between federal soldiers and Indians between 1798 and 1898, but admits there are hundreds more undocumented between Indians and state troopers, posses, and Texas Rangers (133). And there are no estimates for the total number of skirmishes between pioneers and Indians or Mexicans, but Hollon assumes they would number in the thousands.

5. An excellent source for a full discussion of New Western History is Limerick, Milner, and Rankin's *Trails: Toward a New Western History.*

Chapter 4.
Western Myths in *All the Pretty Horses* and *The Crossing*

1. Two essays discussing John Grady as a hero figure are Gail Morrison's "*All the Pretty Horses*: John Grady Cole's Expulsion from Paradise" and Dianne Luce's "'When You Wake': John Grady Cole's Heroism in *All the Pretty Horses.*"

2. One theme that unifies the Border Trilogy is the conflict between American pastoralism and the violence of Mexican history, as seen preeminently in Mexico's revolution of 1910–16. In all three novels this revolution is presented as the end

of Mexico's hopes for peace. Those with heroic ideals are executed or die in battle, and with the death of idealists dies their idealism. In *Cities of the Plain,* Mr. Johnson serves as another of the familiar anchorite figures whose recollection illustrates this historical truth: "The executions against the mud walls sprayed with new blood over the dried black of the old and the fine powdered clay sifting down from the bulletholes in the wall after the men had fallen and the slow drift of riflesmoke and the corpses stacked in the streets or piled into the woodenwheeled carretas trundling over the cobbles or over the dirt roads to the nameless graves. . . . The endless riding of horses to their deaths bearing flags or banners or the tentlike tapestries painted with portraits of the Virgin carried on poles into battle as if the mother of God herself were authoress of all that calamity and mayhem and madness" (64–65).

Chapter 5.
Thematic Motifs in *Cities of the Plain*

1. Corridos are discussed at length in Americo Paredes's *With His Pistol in His Hand, A Texas-Mexican Cancionero,* and *Folklore and Culture.* Together these books form a comprehensive trilogy on the Mexican ballad. Paredes notes that the orality of corridos keeps the details of any particular ballad fresh, as it changes with each retelling. The oldest corrido to be handed down is from the 1860s and involves a Texas cattle drive. Themes of conflict fill the corridos of the borderlands, as ethnic conflicts generate violence.

Works Cited

Ahnebrink, Lars. *The Beginnings of Naturalism in American Fiction: A Study of the Works of Hamlin Garland, Stephen Crane, and Frank Norris.* New York: Russell, 1961.

Aldridge, John W. "Cormac McCarthy's Bizarre Genius." *Atlantic Monthly* 274 (1994): 89.

Allmendinger, Blake. *The Cowboy.* New York: Oxford University Press, 1992.

Anderson, Sherwood. *Winesburg, Ohio.* New York: Viking, 1960.

Arnold, Edwin T. "Blood and Grace: The Fiction of Cormac McCarthy." *Commonweal* 4 Nov. 1994: 11–16.

—————. "Naming, Knowing and Nothingness: McCarthy's Moral Parables." Arnold and Luce 43–68.

Arnold, Edwin T., and Dianne C. Luce, eds. *Perspectives on Cormac McCarthy.* Jackson: University Press of Mississippi, 1993.

Athearn, Robert G. *The Mythic West in Twentieth-Century America.* Lawrence: University Press of Kansas, 1986.

Beidler, Philip D. *Rewriting America: Vietnam Authors in Their Generation.* Athens: University of Georgia Press, 1991.

Bell, Vereen. *The Achievement of Cormac McCarthy.* Baton Rouge: Louisiana State University Press, 1988.

—————. "The Ambiguous Nihilism of Cormac McCarthy." *Southern Literary Journal* 15 (1983): 31–41.

—————. "'Between the Wish and the Thing the World Lies Waiting.'" *Southern Review* 28 (1992): 920–27.

Bergson, Henri. *Laughter: An Essay on the Meaning of the Comic.* Trans. Cloudesley Brereton. New York: Macmillan, 1911.

Bidney, David. "Myth, Symbolism, and Truth." *Myth and Literature.* Ed. John B. Vickery. Lincoln: University of Nebraska Press, 1966. 3–13.

Bierce, Ambrose. "Chickamauga." *Ambrose Bierce's Civil War.* Ed. William McCann. New York: Wings, 1956. 99–107.

Bingham, Arthur. "Syntactic Complexity and Iconicity in Cormac McCarthy's *Blood Meridian*." *Language and Literature* 20 (1995): 19–33.

Busby, Mark. "The Significance of the Frontier." Mogen, Busby, and Bryant 95–106.

Butler, Anne M. "Selling the Popular Myth." Milner, O'Connor, and Sandweiss 771–801.

Campbell, Joseph. *Myths to Live By*. New York: Viking, 1972.

Cawelti, John G. "Cormac McCarthy: Restless Seekers." *Southern Writers at Century's End*. Ed. Jeffrey J. Folks and James H. Justus. Lexington: University Press of Kentucky, 1997. 164–76.

Civello, Paul. *American Literary Naturalism and Its Twentieth-Century Transformations: Frank Norris, Ernest Hemingway, and Don DeLillo*. Athens: University of Georgia Press, 1994.

Crane, Stephen. *The Complete Short Stories and Sketches of Stephen Crane*. Ed. Thomas A. Gullason. Garden City, NY: Doubleday, 1963.

———. *The Red Badge of Courage and Other Stories*. New York: Dodd, Mead, 1957.

Dary, David. *Cowboy Culture: A Saga of Five Centuries*. Lawrence: University Press of Kansas, 1989.

Daugherty, Leo. "Gravers False and True: *Blood Meridian* as Gnostic Tragedy." Arnold and Luce 157–72.

The Dellums Committee Hearings on War Crimes in Vietnam: An Inquiry into Command Responsibility in Southeast Asia. New York: Vintage, 1972.

Dickey, James. *Babel to Byzantium: Poets and Poetry Now*. New York: Grosset and Dunlap, 1968.

———. *Deliverance*. Boston: Houghton Mifflin, 1970.

Donoghue, Denis. "Dream Work." *New York Review of Books* 24 June 1993: 5–10.

Ehrenreich, Barbara. *Blood Rites*. New York: Metropolitan, 1997.

Eisler, Riane. *The Chalice and the Blade: Our History, Our Future*. San Francisco: Harper, 1988.

Evenson, Brian. "McCarthy's Wanderers: Nomadology, Violence, and Open Country." Hall and Wallach 41–48.

Faragher, John Mack, Mari Jo Buhle, Daniel Czitrom, and Susan H. Armitage. *Out of Many: A History of the American People*. Englewood Cliffs, NJ: Prentice Hall, 1994.

Faulkner, William. *The Hamlet*. New York: Vintage, 1959.

Fehrenbach, T. R. *Comanches: The Destruction of a People*. New York: Knopf, 1974.

Frost, Robert. *Collected Poems of Robert Frost*. New York: Buccaneer, 1986.

WORKS CITED

Fukuyama, Francis. *The End of History and the Last Man.* New York: Free Press; New York: Macmillan, 1992.

Girard, René. *Violence and the Sacred.* Baltimore: Johns Hopkins University Press, 1977.

Gross, Theodore L. *The Heroic Ideal in American Literature.* New York: Free Press, 1971.

Hall, Wade. "The Hero as Philosopher and Survivor: An Afterword on *The Stonemason* and *The Crossing*." Hall and Wallach 189–94.

———. "The Human Comedy of Cormac McCarthy." Hall and Wallach 49–60.

Hall, Wade, and Rick Wallach, eds. *Sacred Violence: A Reader's Companion to Cormac McCarthy.* El Paso: Texas Western Press, 1995.

Hemingway, Ernest. *A Moveable Feast: Sketches of the Author's Life in Paris in the Twenties.* New York: Scribner's, 1964.

Hofstadter, Richard, and Michael Wallace. *American Violence: A Documentary History.* New York: Vintage, 1971.

Hollon, W. Eugene. *Frontier Violence: Another Look.* New York: Oxford University Press, 1974.

Hunt, Alexander. "'Strange Equality': A Reading of McCarthy's *Blood Meridian.*" *The Image of the American West in Literature, the Media, and Society.* Ed. Will Wright and Steven Kaplan. Pueblo, CO: Society for the Interdisciplinary Study of Social Imagery, 1996. 237–40.

James, Caryn. "Is Everyone Dead around Here?" *New York Times Book Review* 28 April 1985: 31.

Jarrett, Robert L. *Cormac McCarthy.* New York: Twayne, 1997.

Josyph, Peter. "Blood Music: Reading *Blood Meridian*." Hall and Wallach 169–88.

Kaplan, Robert D. *The Ends of the Earth: A Journey at the Dawn of the 21st Century.* New York: Random House, 1996.

———. "Was Democracy Just a Movement?" *Atlantic Monthly* Dec. 1997: 55–80.

Karnow, Stanley. *Vietnam: A History.* New York: Viking Press, 1983.

Knox, Bernard M. W. *The Heroic Temper: Studies in Sophoclean Tragedy.* Berkeley: University of California Press, 1964.

Kreml, Nancy. "Stylistic Variation and Cognitive Constraint in *All the Pretty Horses.*" Hall and Wallach 137–47.

Kunzig, Robert. "Atapuerca: The Face of an Ancestral Child." *Discover* December 1997: 88–101.

Lewis, R. W. B. *The American Adam.* Chicago: University of Chicago Press, 1955.

Limerick, Patricia Nelson. "The Adventures of the Frontier in the Twentieth Century." *The Frontier in American Culture*. Ed. James R. Grossman. Berkeley: University of California Press, 1994. 67–102.

———. "Borderland vs. Frontier: Redefining the West." *Humanities* Sept.-Oct. 1996: 4–9+.

———. *The Legacy of Conquest: The Unbroken Past of the American West*. New York: W. W. Norton, 1987.

———. "The Persistence of the Frontier." *Harper's* Oct. 1994: 21–24.

Limerick, Patricia Nelson, Clyde A. Milner, and Charles E. Rankin, eds. *Trails: Toward a New Western History*. Lawrence: University Press of Kansas, 1991.

Lopez, Barry Holstun. *Of Wolves and Men*. New York: Charles Scribner's Sons, 1978.

Love, Glen. "Et in Arcadia Ego: Pastoral Theory Meets Ecocriticism." *Western American Literature* 23 (1992): 195–206.

Luce, Dianne C. "On the Trail of History in McCarthy's *Blood Meridian*." *Mississippi Quarterly: The Journal of Southern Culture* 49 (1996): 843–49.

———. "'When You Wake': John Grady Cole's Heroism in *All the Pretty Horses*." Hall and Wallach 155–67.

Lyon, Thomas J. "The Literary West." Milner, O'Connor, and Sandweiss 707–41.

Mailer, Norman. *Advertisements for Myself*. New York: Signet, 1959.

Malone, Michael P., and Richard W. Etulain. *The American West: A Twentieth-Century History*. Lincoln: University Press of Nebraska, 1989.

Marx, Leo. "Contrasting Versions of the American Myth." *Open Spaces, City Places*. Ed. Judy Nolte Temple. Tucson: University of Arizona Press, 1994. 39–56.

———. *The Machine in the Garden: Technology and the Pastoral Ideal in America*. New York: Oxford University Press, 1964.

McCarthy, Cormac. *All the Pretty Horses*. New York: Knopf, 1992.

———. *Blood Meridian: Or, The Evening Redness in the West*. New York: Knopf, 1985.

———. *Cities of the Plain*. New York: Knopf, 1998.

———. *The Crossing*. New York: Knopf, 1994.

McCoy, Glen. "The Vietnam War: Not Very Pretty." *Living in America: A Popular Culture Reader*. Ed. Patricia Y. Murray and Scott F. Covell. New York: Mayfield, 1998. 56–60.

Meldrum, Barbara Howard, ed. *Old West–New West: Centennial Essays*. Moscow: University of Idaho Press, 1993.

———. *Under the Sun: Myth and Realism in Western American Literature*. Troy, NY: Whitston, 1985.

Milgram, Stanley. *Obedience to Authority: An Experimental View*. New York: Harper, 1974.
Miller, Frank. *Censored Hollywood: Sex, Sin, and Violence on Screen*. Atlanta: Turner Publications, 1994.
Milner, Clyde A., Carol A. O'Connor, and Martha A. Sandweiss, eds. *The Oxford History of the American West*. New York: Oxford University Press, 1994.
Milowski, Carol Porterfield. *Revisioning the American Frontier: Mary Hallock Foote, Mary Austin, Willa Cather, and the Western Narrative*. Diss. Indiana University of Pennsylvania, 1996.
Mogen, David. *Wilderness Visions: Science Fiction Westerns*. Vol. 1. San Bernardino, CA: Borgo Press, 1982.
Mogen, David, Mark Busby, and Paul Bryant, eds. *The Frontier Experience and the American Dream: Essays on American Literature*. College Station: Texas A&M University Press, 1989.
Mogen, David, Scott P. Sanders, and Joanne B. Karpinski, eds. *Frontier Gothic: Terror and Wonder at the Frontier in American Literature*. Rutherford, NJ: Fairleigh Dickinson University Press, 1993.
Morgan, Terrence. "The Wired West." *The New Republic* 6 May 1985: 37–38.
Morrison, Gail Moore. "*All the Pretty Horses*: John Grady Cole's Expulsion from Paradise." Arnold and Luce 173–93.
Moyer, K. E. *Violence and Aggression: A Physiological Perspective*. New York: Paragon, 1987.
Moyers, Bill. "Conquering America: Bharati Mukherjee." *A World of Ideas*. Videorecording. Princeton, N.J.: Films for the Humanities, 1994.
Nash, Roderick. *Wilderness and the American Mind*. New Haven: Yale University Press, 1967.
Noble, David W. *The Eternal Adam and the New World Garden: The Central Myth in the American Novel Since 1830*. New York: George Braziller, 1968.
Nolan, Tom. Rev. of *Blood Meridian*, by Cormac McCarthy. *Los Angeles Times Book Review* 9 June 1985: B2.
Norris, Frank. *McTeague*. New York: Penguin, 1982.
O'Brien, Tim. *The Things They Carried*. New York: Penguin, 1990.
Palmer, Louis H. *The Use of the Double or Doppelgänger in the Novels of Cormac McCarthy*. Thesis. Appalachian State University, 1991.
Paredes, Americo, ed. *Folklore and Culture on the Texas-Mexican Border*. Austin: University of Texas, 1993.
———. *A Texas-Mexican Cancionero: Folksongs of the Lower Border*. Chicago: University of Illinois Press, 1976.

———. "*With His Pistol in His Hand*": *A Border Ballad and Its Hero*. Austin: University of Texas Press, 1958.

Parrish, Tim. "The Killer Wears the Halo: Cormac McCarthy, Flannery O'Connor, and the American Religion." Hall and Wallach 25–40.

Peterson, Charles S. "Speaking for the Past." Milner, O'Connor, and Sandweiss 743–69.

Peterson, James R. "Playboy's History of the Sexual Revolution: Part VII—1960–1969: Make Love Not War." *Playboy* June 1998: 86+.

Phillips, Dana. "History and the Ugly Facts of Cormac McCarthy's *Blood Meridian*." *American Literature* 68 (1996): 433–60.

Pilkington, Tom. "Fate and Free Will on the American Frontier: Cormac McCarthy's Western Fiction." *Western American Literature* 24 (1993): 311–20.

Pitts, Jonathan. "Writing On: *Blood Meridian* as Devisionary Western." *Western American Literature* 33 (1998): 7–25.

Pizer, Donald, ed. *The Cambridge Companion to American Realism and Naturalism: Howells to London*. Cambridge: Cambridge University Press, 1995.

———. *Realism and Naturalism in Nineteenth-Century American Literature*. Carbondale: Southern Illinois University Press, 1966.

———. *The Theory and Practice of American Literary Naturalism: Selected Essays and Reviews*. Carbondale: Southern Illinois University Press, 1993.

———. *Twentieth-Century American Literary Naturalism: An Interpretation*. Carbondale: Southern Illinois University Press, 1982.

Pratt, John Clark. "The Lost Frontier: American Myth in the Literature of the Vietnam War." Mogen, Busby and Bryant 236–47.

Pope, Alexander. "Epistle to Dr. Arbuthnot." *The Complete Poetical Works of Pope*. Boston: Houghton Mifflin, 1903. 176–82.

———. "An Essay on Man." *The Complete Poetical Works of Pope*. Boston: Houghton Mifflin, 1903. 137–55.

Robertson, James Oliver. *American Myth, American Reality*. New York: Hill and Wang, 1980.

Robinson, Cecil. *No Short Journeys: The Interplay of Cultures in the History and Literature of the Borderlands*. Tucson: University of Arizona Press, 1992.

Robinson, Forrest G. "The New Historicism and the Old West." Meldrum, *Old West* 74–96.

Schlosser, Eric. "A Grief Like No Other." *Atlantic Monthly* September 1997: 37–76.

Schopen, Bernard A. "'They Rode On': *Blood Meridian* and the Art of Narrative." *Western American Literature* 25 (1994): 179–93.

Sepich, John Emil. *Notes on "Blood Meridian."* Louisville: Bellarmine College Press, 1993.
Shaviro, Steven. "'The Very Life of Darkness': A Reading of *Blood Meridian.*" Arnold and Luce 143–56.
Shaw, Patrick W. "The Kid's Fate, the Judge's Guilt: Ramification of Closure in Cormac McCarthy's *Blood Meridian.*" *Southern Literary Journal* 30 (1997): 102–19.
Shepard, Sam. *Cruising Paradise.* New York: Knopf, 1996.
Slatta, Richard. *Bandidos: The Varieties of Latin America Banditry.* New York: Greenwood, 1987.
———. *Cowboys of the Americas.* New Haven: Yale University Press, 1990.
Slotkin, Richard. *The Fatal Environment.* New York: Atheneum, 1985.
———. *Gunfighter Nation: The Myth of the Frontier in Twentieth-Century America.* New York: Atheneum, 1992.
———. *Regeneration through Violence.* Middletown, CT: Wesleyan University Press, 1973.
Smith, Henry Nash. *Virgin Land.* 2nd ed. Cambridge, MA: Harvard University Press, 1971.
Spencer, William Christopher. *The Extremities of Cormac McCarthy: The Major Character Types.* Diss. University of Tennessee, Knoxville, 1993.
Steinbeck, John. "The Leader of the People." *The Portable Steinbeck.* Ed. Pascal Covici, Jr. New York: Penguin, 1976. 397–416.
Stone, Robert, and Julene Fischer. *Images of War: A Vietnam Portfolio.* Boston: Boston Publishing, 1986.
Sussman, Robert W. "Exploring Our Basic Human Nature: Are Humans Inherently Violent?" *Anthro Notes* Fall 1997: 1–8+.
Turner, Frederick. *Of Chiles, Cacti, and Fighting Cocks: Notes on the American West.* San Francisco: North Point Press, 1990.
———. *Spirit of Place: The Making of an American Literary Landscape.* San Francisco: Sierra Club Books, 1989.
Twain, Mark. *The Adventures of Huckleberry Finn.* New York: Harper, 1987.
Uruburu, Paula M. *The Gruesome Doorway: An Analysis of the American Grotesque.* New York: Peter Lang, 1987.
Wallach, Rick. "Judge Holden: *Blood Meridian*'s Evil Archon." Hall and Wallach 125–36.
West, Elliot. "American Frontier." Milner, O'Connor and Sandweiss 115–50.
———. Foreword. Athearn ix–xi.
Westbrook, Max. "Myth, Reality, and the American Frontier." Meldrum, *Under the Sun* 10–19.

Westbrook, Perry D. *Free Will and Determinism in American Literature*. Cranbury, NJ: Associated University Presses, 1979.

Whitman, Walt. *Leaves of Grass*. San Francisco: Chandler, 1968.

Wills, Gary. "The American Adam." *New York Review of Books* 6 March 1997: 30–33.

Winchell, Mark. "Inner Dark: Or, The Place of Cormac McCarthy." *Southern Review* 25 (1990): 293–309.

The Winter Soldier Investigation: An Inquiry into American War Crimes. Boston: Beacon Press, 1972.

Witek, Terri. "Reeds and Hides: Cormac McCarthy's Domestic Spaces." *Southern Review* 30 (1994): 136–42.

Woodward, Richard B. "Cormac McCarthy's Venomous Fiction." *New York Times Magazine* 19 April 1992: 28–31+.

Wrangham, Richard W. "Apes, Culture, and the Missing Links." *Symbols* Spring 1995: 2–9+.

Wrangham, Richard W., and Dale Peterson. *Demonic Males: Apes and the Origins of Human Violence*. Boston: Houghton Mifflin, 1996.

Wright, James. *Collected Poems*. Middletown, CT: Wesleyan University Press, 1972.

Wright, Will. *Sixguns and Society: A Structural Study of the Western*. Berkeley: University of California Press, 1975.

Young, Thomas D., Jr. "Cormac McCarthy and the Geology of Being." *DAI* 51 (1990): 2022A.

Zimbardo, Philip G. "A Pirandellian Prison." *New York Times Magazine* 8 April 1973: 38–40.

About the Author

Barcley Owens earned his Ph.D. in American Studies at Washington State University in 1997. He teaches composition and American literature at Big Bend Community College, located in the volcanic barrens of the Columbia Basin in eastern Washington. A writer of short fiction himself, he considers Cormac McCarthy "the century's last great male writer in the tradition of London, Hemingway, Mailer, and Dickey."